Stones, Bones and Gods

Discovering the beliefs of primitive man in Britain

R.T. Pearce

Ward Lock Educational

ISBN 0 7062 4041 3

First published 1982

Computer type-set in 11 on 12 point Times Roman
by Page Bros (Norwich) Ltd
Printed by Chigwell Press,
Buckhurst Hill, Essex
for Ward Lock Educational Company Limited
47 Marylebone Lane, London W1M 6AX
A Ling Kee company

Contents

Acknowledgments

Grateful thanks are due to the following for permission to
reproduce illustrations: Aerofilms, Stonehenge p.31; Janet and
Colin Bord, p.17, p.19, p.24, p.25, p.27, West Kennet Avenue
p.31, p.33, maypole p.45, Long Man of Wilmington p.49, p.54,
p.62, p.64, p.65, p.77, p.87, p.89; by courtesy of the Trustees of
the British Museum, Grimes Graves figurine p.12; Department of
the Environment (Crown Copyright reserved), p.21; Michael
Holford, standing woman figurine p.12; Mansell Collection,
Astarte p.45; Museum of London, p.9; National Museum,
Copenhagen, rim of bowl p.56; John Topham Picture Library,
p.11, stone head p.56. The diagram on p.37 is after a diagram
from *Megalithic Sites in Britain*, A. Thom, published by Oxford
University Press (1967). Picture research: Faith Perkins.

Introduction

This book is about the beliefs of men and women living in Britain from earliest times until the coming of Christianity. For much of the time people could not read or write so we have only the things they left behind to consider when we try to discover their beliefs.

We will be looking at the ideas which men and women had about themselves and their place in the world. We shall discover the powers and gods on which early people believed themselves to be dependent and also their thoughts about life after death. Unusual paintings and carvings were left by these early communities, and their great monuments still remain on our hillsides today.

Through clues left on the landscape and hints from the remains of the settlements we can guess at ceremonies and religious rites observed by these early people. Why, for example, were their graves so big? West Kennet Long Barrow is over 100 metres long. Imagine all the effort needed to build a mound of earth as long as a football pitch and as high and wide as a classroom: what beliefs could have urged Stone Age men and women to this extent?

Throughout the book, historical background information is given where necessary. Special words are occasionally used and their meanings can be checked in the glossary at the end of the book. For project work and further study, references are given to articles in Encyclopaedia Britannica, which should be available in your school or local library. There is a lot of information about places to visit, some of which may not be very far away from your home or school.

Time Chart

Lower and Middle Old Stone Age (Lower and Middle Palaeolithic)	From the appearance of man-like creatures to about 38,000 BC	Over this very long period of time the climate changed several times from very cold to warm. Sea level rose as much as 30 metres and dropped as much as 100 metres.
Upper Old Stone Age (Upper Palaeolithic)	From about 38,000 BC to about 8500 BC	The species to which we belong (*Homo Sapiens*) appeared about 38,000 BC. He wore skins, hunted with flint weapons, did cave paintings and carved bone and stone. He reverently buried the dead. Climate cold; bison and mammoth in Britain
Middle Stone Age (Mesolithic)	From about 8500 BC to about 4000 BC	Weather began to improve. Big animals moved away or died. Man hunted and fished, wore skins and lived in simple shelters. Sea level rose almost to present level about 5000 BC
New Stone Age (Neolithic)	From about 4000 BC to about 2000 BC	Discovery of agriculture and farming; invention of pottery; Megalithic religious monuments, long barrows, gallery graves, passage graves, stone circles, polished stone tools
Bronze Age	From about 2000 BC to about 800 BC	Weaving, metal (copper, tin, gold) used for tools, weapons, pots, jewels; round barrows
Iron Age	From about 800 BC to AD 43 when the Romans came and conquered the Celts.	Iron tools and weapons; hill-forts; wheel-turned pottery; druids

1 Cave Men and Hunters

Imagine you have been taken back in time to the Old Stone Age, about 20,000 years before the birth of Christ. You are watching a small group of men making their way up a mountain track by the side of a river. The weather is cold and the men are wearing animal skins. They are carrying an assortment of objects. One has a small oil lamp and some pieces of flint, another has a shell filled to the brim with paint and a third carries small bundles of sticks and some longer pieces of wood. At the base of high limestone cliffs the men pause and then enter the low mouth of a cave. Almost immediately they descend the steep narrow passage leading into the mountain.

After nearly an hour they are still making their way into the heart of the mountain with only the smoky flame of the oil lamp to show the way. Sometimes the cave is wide and high and they cannot see the roof; at other times it is so low and narrow that they have to crawl along. In places there are deep pools of water which are fed by noisy waterfalls. Eventually they stop, place their equipment on the ground and begin to paint. One draws the outline of a large bison; another colours the body of a deer which he had already started; the third man makes some black marks on the bodies of some of the animals.

Later on, when the supply of paint has run out, the men begin their slow journey back to the entrance. Their work will not be seen by most of their friends because it is too far from the mouth of the cave. It will not be seen again for thousands of years. Why did they bother? What was it all about? These are questions which archaeologists ask, and the answers they give are clues to the religious beliefs of early man.

The Stone Ages

In this book we are concerned only with *Homo Sapiens*. These two Latin words mean 'wise man' and together they form the term given to modern man, the species to which we all belong. From the evidence available we think that *Homo Sapiens* appeared about 40,000 years ago. From then until about 2000 BC men and women used only stone, bone and wood for their tools and weapons. This long period of time is called the Stone Age, but because man's skills and stone-using techniques changed, it is usually divided into three separate periods:

1 Old Stone Age
2 Middle Stone Age
3 New Stone Age

There were man-like creatures on the earth long before *Homo Sapiens* and they used stone tools as well. To distinguish between their history and the history of *Homo Sapiens*, we say that these man-like creatures lived in the Lower and Middle Old Stone Ages, whereas modern man lived in the Upper Old Stone Age. There was, of course, no sudden change from one period to another and these man-like creatures, for example Neanderthal Man, would have lived alongside *Homo Sapiens*. We do not yet know the precise relationship between them.

The names of these Stone Ages are usually given in their Greek form. If you learn five Greek words, you will have no difficulty in translating them.

palaios	–	old
mesos	–	middle
neos	–	new
lithos	–	stone
megas	–	big

Palaeolithic means 'Old Stone' and Megalithic means 'Big Stone', the name given to the massive stone monuments like Stonehenge.

For the dates of these periods of man's history see the Time Chart at the beginning of this book.

Upper Old Stone Age
From about 38,000 BC to about 8000 BC life was difficult for man. For much of the time the climate was cold and large parts of the country were covered with ice. Sea level was as much as 100 metres lower than it is now, and men could freely walk over to Ireland in one direction and to the continent in the other. There were few of the trees we see today and fierce animals, such as bison and woolly rhinoceros, roamed about. Men and women wore skins and spent much of their time hunting these animals for food or protecting themselves from them. Their tools were made of flint and the most common tool was the hand-axe.

Middle Stone Age

When the climate began to improve about 8000 BC everything else began to change. The water trapped in the form of ice began to melt and the sea level slowly began to rise. By 6000 BC it was about twenty metres below the present level and by 5500 BC it was seven metres below present levels. The land-bridge to the continent was flooded and thousands of people had to move to higher ground. Settlements were abandoned and their remains now lie many miles out to sea.

The warmer climate brought new types of vegetation and animal life. The big ferocious animals died out and became extinct. Man had to find new kinds of food and develop new types of flint tools and weapons. In many coastal areas today, for instance, there are thick layers of shells which can be dated from the Middle Stone Age. They were the rubbish-tips of ancient settlements.

Mesolithic camp,
c. 5000 BC.

Stone Age Religion

Religion has to do with the beliefs men and women have about the mysterious forces which seem to influence their lives. It also involves the things people do in an attempt to win the support of these forces. When we try to find out about Stone Age religion, however, we face a problem because Stone Age man left no written information about his beliefs. We can only guess what these beliefs were by looking carefully at what he did leave.

In this section we shall consider the things which were left by people of the Upper Old Stone Age and the Middle Stone Age. In later chapters we shall be looking at evidence from the New Stone Age. Firstly, we shall think about the cave paintings of the Upper Old Stone Age. These are the earliest examples of art ever found and it seems clear that they are connected with religious beliefs. Nobody would ever paint pictures in remote parts of dark caves if they were simply for decoration. Secondly, we shall consider the carvings from this period, some of which have been found in caves. Finally, we will look at the way the dead were buried. *Homo Sapiens* has buried the dead reverently at all stages of his development and Middle Stone Age graves are similar to those of the Upper Old Stone Age. The care taken and the objects buried with the body tell us much about early man's religion.

Paintings

In caves in south-western Europe, especially in the mountains between France and Spain, there are colourful paintings of animals from the Upper Old Stone Age. Most of the animals are now extinct. As far as we know, no one had ever painted before and so paint, brushes and lamps had to be made. Man probably used powdered rock and water for paint just like the Australian aborigines of today. Brushes may have been made from chewed sticks or feathers.

These early people went to a lot of trouble to do the paintings. Some of them are located deep in the caves more than a mile from the entrance. Others are on the high ceilings of the caves and ladders of some kind would have been needed to reach them. Quite often they are in places where the painter would have been wedged between rough surfaces of rock with hardly any space to move.

Nearly all the paintings are of animals like bison, deer, horses and bulls. About fifteen per cent of the animals are wounded with

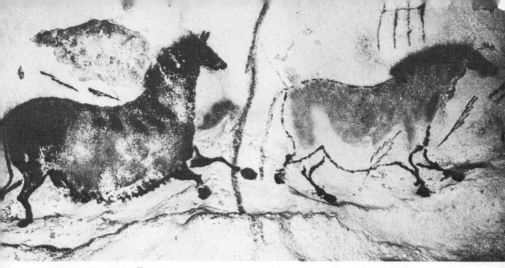

Cave paintings, Lascaux, France.

spears and arrows. Many of the others look pregnant, but none of these animals are wounded. There are a few human figures, but they look strange alongside the animals.

At this stage in man's history, men and women had not learnt how to grow their own crops. They depended on their skill as hunters for food. This is why we think that the paintings were an attempt to make the hunting trips successful. They probably hoped that by some kind of magic the animals wounded in the paintings would be wounded in real life. The pregnant animals were left untouched because they knew that they needed a constant supply of animals in order to survive.

The human figures are puzzling. Some of them have animal heads. We cannot know for certain what they were doing, but the customs of North American Plains Indians may give us some ideas. On the night before a hunt the Sioux and Cheyenne did a buffalo dance dressed in the skins and heads of buffalo. Perhaps the Stone Age men were dancing? On the other hand, warriors of the Cherokee and Tuscarora tribes wore animal skins and heads while they were actually hunting. In this disguise they could creep up on grazing animals without being noticed.

The animal paintings are colourful and realistic; the human figures look like matchstick men. It is as though the painters were showing their admiration for these powerful animals which made them feel weak and helpless. If this is so, then these paintings would be acts of worship. They would be giving value and worth to the animals who were stronger and on whom man depended for life.

Venus figurines: *above*, from Grimes Graves, Brandon, Suffolk; *left*, from Catal Huyuk, Turkey.

Carvings

Stone Age men and women were very good at making tools and weapons. Anyone who has tried to make an arrow head from a piece of flint will know that it is not easy. It takes much patience and skill. They were also good at carving and engraving pieces of stone and bone. They carved many kinds of objects, but two in particular were very popular: animals and fat women.

The animals may have been carved for the same reason that they were painted, but the fat women seem to have served a different purpose. Archaeologists call them 'Venuses' and they seem to be connected with child-birth. The small statues have fat bodies and either very thin arms or no arms at all. Most of them have no facial features, but some of them have a mass of hair. Their legs are short and sometimes taper to a point as if the statues were stuck in the ground. They may have been ornaments or decorations, but it seems more likely that they were religious objects connected with birth and fertility. They may have been placed near a woman who was expecting a baby so that the baby would be born alive. In those days many babies died during birth or soon afterwards.

Graves

Animals use the dead bodies of other animals for food. Amongst human beings, however, cannibalism is rare. From the earliest times men and women have buried their dead with the greatest of care. In the Old Stone Age some were buried as if they were sleeping; others were buried in a crouching position with the knees folded close to the chest. As this is the position taken by a baby before it is born, it may have been used in the hope that the dead person would be re-born in some way. On the other hand, in some tribes today dead bodies are tied up so that their spirit will not haunt the camp or village and this may have been the reason. In either case there is a belief in a life after death.

Sometimes bodies were buried with animal bones, horns or tusks near to them. This may have been food for the dead person, but it may also have been something to do with the strength of the animal. Men have sometimes thought that the strength of an animal was concentrated in the horns or antlers. Perhaps they believed that this strength could be passed on to human beings?

Dead bodies were also given tools and ornaments. Around 28,000 BC, for example, adults and children were buried with necklaces, pendants, hairpins and flint tools. One child even had its own tiny implements close to its body. They were beautifully made miniatures which had been provided specially for the burial. Such a level of care for the dead body of a relative or friend shows the high value which was placed on the human being.

Another unusual custom of burial in the Stone Age period was the covering of the body with a powder called red ochre. This stained everything red and made the body look as if it was soaked in blood. Perhaps this was done because people thought blood had life-giving power and they wanted the corpse to live again?

Conclusion
Human beings and animals are similar in many respects. If you compare the skeleton of a man with that of an ape, you will see how much alike they are. There are, however, many differences between human beings and animals. First, man has the ability to make things and invent things. No animal has ever painted a picture like those in the caves of southern Europe. Secondly, he can use symbols and communicate ideas. No animals can do this. Thirdly, he is able to think about his past and prepare for his future. This is one of the reasons why religion has developed. Men and women have come to realize that they depend on powers beyond themselves and they want to get to know these powers and win their support.

Revision Exercise

1 Name the three materials used for making tools and weapons during the Stone Age.
2 Give the dates for the part of the Old Stone Age when *Homo Sapiens* lived in Europe.
3 When did the climate begin to change in Europe and the Middle Stone Age begin?
4 Name three kinds of evidence which give us clues to the religious beliefs of men and women in the Stone Age.
5 What evidence is there that Stone Age man believed in a life after death?

Things to Do

1 Find out what you can about the climate and sea-level during the Stone Age period. If you live near the seaside, try to work out how far away the coastline would have been in about 10,000 BC.
2 Draw and colour animals like those found in the cave paintings. You should have several books in the school library which have photographs of the paintings. Look in the Art section as well as the History section.
3 Try to assemble a display of postage stamps showing cave and rock paintings. The following are listed with their Stanley Gibbons Simplified Catalogue numbers:
Australia, 1971, Aboriginal Art: Cave Painting, 496
France, 1968, French Art Series, 1786
Guernsey, 1977, Prehistoric Monuments, 153–156
Spain, 1967, Wall Painting Set, 1837–46

Encyclopaedia Britannica, **Articles for Further Study**
'Ancient Britain', Macropaedia, Vol. 3, pp. 193—197
'Ancient Europe', Macropaedia, Vol. 6, pp. 1059–1066
'Arts of Stone Age Peoples', Macropaedia, Vol. 17, pp. 702–708
'Ceremonial and Ritualistic Objects', Macropaedia, Vol. 3, pp. 1174–1182
'Feasts and Festivals', Macropaedia, Vol. 7, 197–202
'Prehistoric Religion', Macropaedia, Vol. 14, 984–989

2 Farmers of the New Stone Age

Around 4000 BC in Britain an amazing revolution took place.
Man's whole way of life changed. People began to plant their
own crops, keep their own cattle and sheep and make pottery.
The constant search for food of the Middle Stone Age had come
to an end and the New Stone Age began.

These new discoveries meant that there was more time
available for other activities. Men found that they could polish
flint and stone tools, for instance. They also decorated their
pottery and you can probably see examples of New Stone Age
pottery in your local museum.

As farmers they soon realized that they needed ways of
keeping track of the seasons so that they would know when to
plant their seeds. They needed some kind of calendar and after
careful observations of the movements of the sun, moon and
stars, they came to see that these were connected with the
changes in the seasons. Summer was at its height, for example,
when the sun rose at its most northerly point. After that, when
the sun rose a little further south each day, they knew that winter
was on its way.

They also needed to know when the growing season was ending
so that they could kill off most of their cattle for food through the
winter. At such times there would be great rejoicing and they
would thank the gods upon whom they depended.

One of the most impressive features of the New Stone Age was
the building of megaliths. These were the massive stone
monuments which are found all over Europe today. Some of
them were graves, but others were more like temples for religious
ceremonies. In this chapter we shall concentrate on the graves
and we shall divide them into five types. Most of them are
impressive and there may be some near where you live.

1 Long Barrows

If you go to visit a long barrow you may be disappointed at first.
In fact, you may find one marked on a map and then be unable
to locate it because it is overgrown with grass and weeds. This is
because many of these long mounds of earth have eroded away in

the six thousand years since they were made. Their construction is impressive.

Imagine the scene: a chief has died and the tribe is preparing for his burial. First a team of men with stone axes is sent to fell trees. They are going to need about two hundred trees with trunks about fifteen centimetres in diameter. The trees are then stripped of branches and cut into three metre lengths. An area of ground is cleared and the stakes are driven into the ground side-by-side to form a long rectangular enclosure. One of the men in charge of the work has made sure that the enclosure lies in an east–west direction.

When the stakes are firmly set in the ground, the body of the chief is placed at the eastern end in a small wooden structure that looks a bit like a small house. By his side are placed some tools, weapons and a pot of grain. The whole enclosure is then filled with chalk rubble dug from the side of a nearby hill. The digging is tedious and hard because the two hundred men involved have only picks made from the antlers of deer and small wicker baskets to carry the rubble. As they empty their baskets into the enclosure there is another team of men whose job is raking the chalk level. After several weeks there is a gleaming white mound about forty metres long and tapered towards the western end.

Long barrows are often very long. It is not unusual to find them over a hundred metres long. In the past people have been puzzled by their size and sometimes they thought they were the graves of giants. Also, for their size they contain very few burials; some long mounds do not have any burials at all. This seems to suggest that the people chosen for this kind of burial must have been very important.

The orientation of the barrows varies slightly from place to place, but most of them lie in an east–west position. The bodies are nearly always placed at the eastern end of the mound with the entrance to the grave facing the rising sun. They probably did this so that the life-giving rays of the sun would shine where the body was.

Experiments have shown that the mounds of chalk stay white for many years. A long white mound on the top of a green hill would have looked an impressive sight. The community may have built them to impress others in the same way that some civic buildings today are built to impress. They may also have been centres for some kind of religious ritual.

2 Single Burial Chambers

In rocky parts of the country some of the long barrows have stone structures to house the bodies instead of wooden ones. Generally speaking, however, the earliest stone tombs are the single burial chambers, sometimes called *dolmens* or 'table stones'. They consist of a flat slab of stone supported by three or more standing stones. Some of them seem to have been once covered with a mound of earth or pile of stones. In most cases, however, the mound has disappeared, leaving the slab delicately poised on slender fingers of stone.

Building these monuments took great strength and skill. It is easy to look at them and not realize how heavy they are. There is one on Anglesey, for example, with a slab six metres long, five metres wide and a metre thick. This enormous capstone must weigh over twenty tonnes, and yet it is supported by slim upright stones which look like pointed teeth. The difficulty involved in moving and lifting a block of stone heavier than a double-decker bus was great.

Most dolmens are in the west of Britain, although they can sometimes be found in areas where you might not expect them. Kits Coty House, for example, near Aylesford in Kent, is less than thirty miles from London.

Lanyon Quoit burial chamber, Madron, Cornwall.

3   Gallery Graves

This name is given to stone burial chambers which are inside long barrows. They are long stone tunnels made from two rows of upright stones with slabs resting on them to form the roof. The gaps between the upright stones are sometimes filled with dry-walling made of small pieces of stone. The roof is the same height from the entrance to the wider burial chamber at the end.

The largest and most famous gallery grave in Europe is West Kennet Long Barrow, situated a few miles west of Marlborough in Wiltshire. The big stone chamber with its five separate compartments is set in a chalk mound which is over a hundred metres long. It is made from the type of sandstone which lies scattered over the rolling downland nearby. The dry-walling, however, between the big upright stones comes from the limestone hills around Frome, twenty-five miles away.

Excavations have shown that about twenty adults and ten children were buried in the tomb's five chambers. They were not all buried at once, but over many years. Some of the skeletons do not have skulls and from the arrangement of the bones it looks as if older bones were pushed to one side when a new burial took place.

Gallery graves usually contain an assortment of objects which were buried with the bodies. These include pots of food and tools and weapons. Some of them also have large quantities of broken pottery and charcoal which may have been offerings either to the gods or to the dead ancestors.

It seems strange to worship dead ancestors and yet this is practised in some parts of the world today. There are two possible reasons for the custom: firstly the offerings may be an attempt to keep the spirits away; secondly, they may be given so that the power of the dead can be called on to help at the time of birth or marriage or sickness. It is possible that megalithic tombs were places where primitive man thought that he could store the power of the dead.

4   Passage Graves

Passage graves are the most recent of the Stone Age tombs and they are found all along the Atlantic coast of Europe from Portugal to Scotland. One of the most impressive is at Newgrange in County Meath in Eire; another fine one is near Grouville on the Island of Jersey. It is called *La Hougue Bie* and is featured on one of Jersey's postage stamps.

The main difference between a passage grave and a gallery grave is that the roof of the gallery grave is at the same height thoughout. In the case of the passage grave, there is a fairly low passage which leads to an inner chamber with a high roof. The mound covering the passage grave is also rounder and higher than the long mound of a gallery grave.

The Newgrange tomb has two interesting features. The first is the decoration on many of the stones. It consists of spirals, curves and zig-zags, all of which have been cut into the hard stone. In front of the entrance to the passage there is a beautifully decorated stone which lies horizontally. A vertical line at its centre marks the axis of the tomb and on each side of the line there are several spirals. As the stone faces the east, it is thought that the spirals represent the sun or the moon.

The second interesting feature is a small opening above the entrance to the tomb. It looks like a tiny window, but once a year its real purpose becomes clear. On the shortest day, the midwinter solstice, light from the rising sun shines through the little opening and along the full length of the passage to the chamber at the end. This shows us that the builders of Newgrange believed that the sun was important to the dead. The arrangement is very similar to the temple of Abu Simbel in Egypt. In this case, the axis of the temple of Rameses II is lined up with the sunrise position of the sun at the equinox. Twice a

Newgrange passage grave, Ireland: the entrance stone.

year the sun's rays penetrate the sixty metre passage and shine on the image of Rameses and Amun, the god of Thebes.

When Newgrange was excavated they found a block of quartz in the tiny window over the entrance. The use of quartz was common in New Stone Age monuments and it seems likely that the builders thought it had special powers.

5 Round Barrows

A barrow is a mound. In the early New Stone Age they built long barrows. At the end of the Stone Age, when men were beginning to make use of copper and tin, the burial mounds were round. In some parts of Britain they are very common and often you can see many of them grouped together. They are usually marked on maps as *tumuli*, and they are sometimes called 'tumps', 'bumps' and 'butts'. The most common type is called a 'bowl barrow' because it looks like an inverted bowl. Others are called bells, discs, saucers and ponds.

Round barrows usually contain only one body, often in a crouching position with a food pot nearby and sometimes with weapons and jewellery. Women seem to have been buried in disc barrows, but these are rare compared with the bowl barrows.

One mound should be specially mentioned, although it is not certain whether it is a barrow or not. This is Silbury Hill, a massive chalk mound near to West Kennet Long Barrow, and the largest man-made mound in Europe. It is forty metres high and has a base diameter of 165 metres. When built it would have been white and very impressive to travellers approaching the area.

Silbury Hill was built to last. It is built on a core of six tiers of chalk blocks, each designed to prevent the chalk rubble from

Section through Bronze Age round barrow, Bamborough, Northumberland.

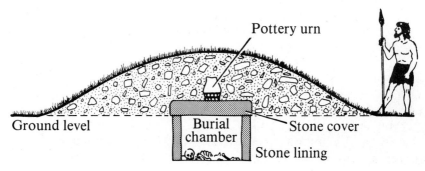

Pottery urn

Ground level Burial chamber Stone cover Stone lining

Aerial view of Silbury Hill, Wiltshire.

sliding down. Archaeologists have estimated that 35,000,000 basket-loads of chalk would have been needed for the mound. This would have taken the labour of 500 men for thirty years.

The hill looks like a burial mound, but no evidence of a burial has been found. There are legends about the burial of a king and so it is possible that his bones might be found one day. On the other hand, it is equally possible that unsupervised labourers found a burial with treasure alongside it and shared the find without telling anybody else about it. This might have happened when Cornish tin miners were employed many years ago to sink a shaft into the hill from the top.

Conclusion

Death is a subject we do not often talk about. Most people die in hospital or on their way to hospital and bodies are rarely kept in the home until the funeral. Our cemeteries are no longer at the centre of our communities and the graveyards of many parish churches have been converted into gardens and the gravestones have been removed. In contrast, prehistoric man made elaborate preparations for burials and the tombs and mounds were prominent features of their settlements. They believed in some kind of life after death because they often buried food pots and tools with the bodies. They may also have had religious ceremonies at the tombs because of their belief in the power the dead had to help the living.

Revision Exercise
1 Name three of the great discoveries of the New Stone Age.
2 How did Stone Age man record the passing of the seasons if he could not write?
3 Why were long barrows built in an east–west direction?
4 How do we know the builders of the Newgrange tomb were sun-worshippers?
5 Suggest reasons why primitive man may have held religious ceremonies at the tombs of his ancestors.

Things to Do
1 Draw elevations of *La Hougue Bie* (height: 13 metres, base: 50 metres), Silbury Hill (height: 40 metres, base: 165 metres), and the largest building in your school, e.g. tower-block, sports hall. Do them all the same scale and put them side by side.
2 See how many *tumuli* you can find on your local Ordnance Survey map. If there are some nearby, arrange a visit.
3 Find out what you can about the Great Pyramid of Cheops or the Temple of Abu Simbel or the passage grave at Newgrange. Note particularly how the sun was important in the design of the monuments. Try to imagine what preparations would be needed before the building of the monuments began.
4 Make clay or plasticine models of the various kinds of round barrows.
5 Study the inscriptions on gravestones in a local cemetery or graveyard and see whether you can detect any changes in attitude to death over the years. You might be able to find old inscriptions on memorials set in the wall of your parish church.

Encyclopaedia Britannica, Articles for Further Study
'Burial Customs and Cults of the Dead', Macropaedia, Vol. 14, p. 985
'Megalithic Tombs', Macropaedia, Vol. 17, p. 707

3 Holy Places

Carlos Castaneda was a student at the University of California in Los Angeles. He was interested in the customs of the Indians who lived in the southern part of Arizona and the northern part of Mexico. In the early 1960s he spent many months with an old Indian called Don Juan. When he had gained the Indian's confidence, he asked him about beliefs and customs and in particular about the use of 'magic mushrooms' – so-called psychedelic mushrooms which have strange effects on those who eat them. It was some time before he was introduced to these things; he first had to find his *sitio*, the place on the ground, according to the Yaqui Indians, which would make him feel different.

For the whole of one night Carlos Castaneda shuffled about the porch of the Indian's house searching for his 'spot'. At first he thought that Don Juan was making a fool of him, but as the hours slowly passed he realized that the search was serious. Eventually he reached a place where things did seem different and he marked the spot with his jacket. He shuffled away from it and noticed that the dim light seemed to change colour. He moved back again and the original colour returned and he seemed to feel happy and refreshed. The whole experience surprised him. Why should he feel different in that particular place? Why should the colour change from green to purple?

To most of us, an experience of this kind seems very odd and we probably assume that it was all in the mind of Castaneda. We think he imagined it, but that it did not really happen. For him, however, and many North American Indians, the idea of special places on the earth's surface makes sense. There are people living in Britain who hold similar beliefs. Some go to Glastonbury and climb to the top of the Tor and claim that they are overcome by a strange feeling and that their mind is filled with questions about the meaning of life and the mystery of human existence. Others claim that they experience the presence of God in churches and cathedrals. If, therefore, these are the feelings some people have now, it seems reasonable to assume that men and women have had these feelings in the past and that there were places where the feelings were strengthened. These are *holy* places.

Glastonbury Tor, Somerset.

A holy place is an area set aside by men and women because they believe that it has some kind of power which other places do not have. It is a place where they think they can make contact with the mysterious forces upon which they feel dependent. It is a place where they want to make some kind of response to these forces.

Throughout Britain there are holy places. Some are on the tops of hills, like Glastonbury Tor; some are by springs and near rivers; others are near unusual natural features such as huge boulders. In this chapter we shall look in some detail at one of these places. It is only a small bump in a field on the island of Anglesey, yet it is one of the most fascinating monuments in Britain.

Bryn Celli Ddu

Bryn Celli Ddu means 'the mound in the dark grove'. It is a passage grave of moderate size standing midway between a large natural boulder and a small river called the Afon Braint. There are no trees near to the mound now and so the view of the Snowdonia mountains across the Menai Straits is impressive.

24

Bryn Celli Ddu passage grave, Llandaniel-Fab, Anglesey.

It looks like a single monument, but it is in fact two monuments on the same spot. The first monument was a circular bank of earth with a ring of stones inside it; the second monument is the passage grave we see today which was built on top of the ring of stones. The builders of the passage grave could have put it anywhere on the island, but they chose this place and had to go to the trouble of breaking up the earlier monument. The reason for this must be that the place was holy.

The Henge
The earlier monument is called a *henge.* This is the name given by archaeologists to a flat circular area surrounded by a bank and ditch. As the ditch is inside the bank, it is obvious that the monument was for ceremonies of some kind and not for defence. Some henges, like this one, had a circle of stones inside the ditch. The most famous henge is Stonehenge, although not every visitor to that monument notices the bank and ditch. There are lesser-known henges in most parts of Britain.

About five thousand years ago, a group of settlers on Anglesey seem to have decided that the little river, now called the Braint, was special. Though only narrow, it is long and a valuable source of fresh water, which was important on a small island. Along its length and never far from the banks they built their sanctuaries. At one end, where it meets the salt water of the Menai Straits opposite Caernarfon, there is a group of standing stones and earthworks. Ten miles away, near its source, there are earthworks, standing stones and a burial chamber. Bryn Celli Ddu lies about half-way between these groups of monuments.

For those who know the story of *Sir Gawain and the Green Knight*, the scene will remind them of the Green Knight's chapel which is described as 'a bulging mound by a bank, beside a stream'. In that story, the Green Knight is a strange god-like figure with mysterious powers. Bryn Celli Ddu gives the visitor the feeling that strange and mysterious things have happened here in the past.

The monument is built around a central pit. In fact, if lines are drawn to join the stones on opposite sides of the monument, they all meet over the pit. It is covered by a large slab of stone and next to the slab there is a long stone covered on three sides with an elaborate pattern of engraved lines. Beneath the slab was a piece of blue clay with a hollowed-out middle and underneath that there was about a metre of soil filling the pit. The soil was carefully sifted and at the bottom of the pit they found one object only: a human ear-bone. The archaeologists were baffled. Not only was it amazing that the entire pit had been dug for such a small bone, but it was equally amazing that Stone Age man knew that this bone existed and that he was able to remove it with flint tools.

Plan of Bryn Celli Ddu showing positions of stones in original circle (a–n).

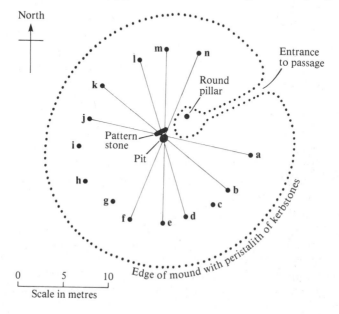

Round pillar inside Bryn Celli Ddu.

The Passage Grave

The builders of the henge either moved away or died out and their place was taken by another group whose monuments were of a different kind. They broke many of the stones of the henge and built a passage grave which they covered with a large mound of earth. The passage is eight metres long and faces north-east, the rising point of the midsummer sun. At the end of the passage there is a hexagonal tomb with a large smooth pillar standing near its centre. The round pillar is about two metres high and gives us a clue to the purpose of the monument. Archaeologists think that it probably represents the male sex organ and that the mound represents a pregnant woman. If this is so, then the monument would have been used for ceremonies which were performed so that the crops would be fertile and that animals and people would reproduce.

Not far from Bryn Celli Ddu there is another passage grave called Barclodiad-y-Gawres ('the Apronful of the Giantess'). It has stones near the entrance which are covered with zig-zags and lozenges and which some take to represent the Mother Goddess. Although the name will have come from a later date, it does help us in our attempt to find out why these monuments were built.

Conclusion

Bryn Celli Ddu is a holy place. It was used by two groups of New Stone Age people and its importance is probably due to its position between the large boulder and the river. Visitors to the monument are conscious of the mysterious nature of the place. Knowing that it was built around a single human ear-bone adds to the mystery. The presence of the pillar inside the mound shows that it was connected with fertility. It was a grave, but it was used for religious ceremonies as well. Perhaps there was a belief in the power of dead ancestors to help the living and men and women came to this place to use that power?

Revision Exercise

1 Say why many ancient religious monuments are built near to rivers.
2 What does the Welsh name Bryn Celli Ddu mean?
3 How do we know that henges were not built for defence?
4 Give three reasons why we know that the central pit was the most important part of the monument.
5 Suggest why a human ear-bone should be buried in this way.

Things to Do

1 Find out what you can about the human ear-bone. It might be necessary to ask a Biology teacher or to look at a Biology text-book.
2 Find out whether there are any henge monuments near to where you live. You can do this by looking at an Ordnance Survey Map. Sometimes they are marked as Earthworks, but their shape is shown as circular. You can check whether they are henges by looking them up in Pevsner's book for your county. (See the list of useful reference books in Chapter 9).
3 Borrow an Ordnance Survey map of Anglesey (Sheet 114) from your public library – they should have a set available for borrowing – and look for ancient monuments close to the River Braint.
4 Check the names of rivers near to you and see whether any of them come from the names of gods. Braint comes from Brigantia, the name of a Celtic river-goddess. London's River Brent also comes from Brigantia.

For Further Study

Craster, E.O. (1953) *Ancient Monuments in Anglesey* (HMSO)

4   Standing Stones

The most fascinating and mysterious Stone Age monuments in Britain are the standing stones. Even though many have been damaged or broken, hundreds of them still remain. There are, in fact, over six hundred groups of stones arranged in rings, as well as hundreds of single stones. Some of them are very big: Stonehenge, for instance, has stones over six metres high. Many others are little more than stumps of stone projecting from the ground. Wherever they are, they raise all kinds of questions about their origin and purpose. With a burial chamber, the purpose is obvious; with a ring of big stones about 400 metres in diameter, as in the case of Avebury, the purpose is a mystery.

Single standing stones are sometimes called *menhirs*. The name means 'long stone' and is one of several words which use the Celtic word *men* or *maen*, 'stone'. *Dolmen*, as we have said, means 'table stone'. *Men-an-tol* means 'stone with a hole in it'. *Men scryfa* means 'inscribed stone'. There are a number of Welsh place-names which include men or maen. Penmaenmawr, for instance, is the town on the Welsh coast near to the Druid's Circle.

The word *lech* or *llech* means a 'dressed stone'. *Cromlech* is derived from it and refers to a ring of standing stones. The word also appears in names of places, like Trelleck, the place in Gwent with three large stones called Harold's Stones.

Folklore
Folklore and tradition have provided us with explanations of the origin of standing stones. One Cornish stone, for instance, is called the Blind Fiddler. According to a local story, the fiddler was playing on a Sunday and, since this was breaking the fourth commandment, he was turned to stone. Not far away there are other sabbath-breakers called the Merry Maidens. Nineteen girls, so the story goes, were dancing to the music of two pipers on a Sunday, and so the whole group was turned to stone. At Stanton Drew in Avon there are three rings called the Weddings. These too were merry-makers condemned because their party went on until Sunday. Other stones have different explanations. The

group to the east of Penrith, for instance, are called Long Meg and Her Daughters. In this case it is black magic which has been punished. All of these stories obviously came into being when the influence of Christianity was widespread.

Rows and Rings
Standing stones can be divided into three categories: first, there are the single standing stones which are isolated from all others. Secondly, there are rows of stones. These may be small tightly-packed rows extending for a hundred metres or so, or well-spaced rows of large stones extending for over a mile, as in the case of Kennet Avenue in Wiltshire. Thirdly, there are the rings. They are sometimes called 'rings' although many of them are not circular, but carefully constructed shapes which have been arranged with amazing accuracy, as we shall see later.

Stonehenge
The best-known stone ring in the world is Stonehenge, near Avesbury in Wiltshire. Each year thousands of visitors go there and many of them are disappointed because it does not seem as big as they had imagined it to be. The trouble is that the stone part of the monument is compact and most visitors take little notice of the rest. It is when one sees the monument as a whole that its size seems impressive.

The first question to be asked about Stonehenge is why it was built on Salisbury Plain. None of the stones come from nearby. Why did they not build a monument where the stones were? Obviously there must have been something special about this particular place. Secondly, how did a group of people who could not write remember all the instructions for so complex a structure? It took many years to build and generations would have come and gone before the monument even began to take shape. What drove them on and made them so keen to build it?

As its name implies, Stonehenge is a henge. The first part to be built was the large circular bank of earth, about 100 metres in diameter. This had to be dug with bone tools and represented many months of hard labour on the part of hundreds of men. Inside the bank there are fifty-six mysterious holes cut into the chalk and then filled with loose rubble. Why fifty-six? Just outside the henge to the north-east they set up a stone which was about three metres high and weighed over thirty tonnes. This stone is still there today and is called the Heel Stone. If you stand at the

Above, West Kennet Avenue, Wiltshire; *below*, aerial view of Stonehenge, Wiltshire.

centre of the monument on midsummer's day, the sun rises above the Heel Stone. This shows clearly that the original henge was connected with the worship of the sun. The fifty-six holes, as we shall see, may be connected with the moon.

The henge was used for over five hundred years without any additional stones. Then, in about 2100 BC, a most remarkable building project began. Teams of men were sent on an overland journey of about two hundred miles to the Presely mountains of Wales. There were no proper roads and no signposts. They had to cross many rivers including the Severn and find their way through miles of thick forest without maps or compasses. Their mission was to cut and shape large blocks of bluestone and bring them back to Salisbury Plain. In all they transported eighty blocks, each of which weighed about four tonnes, the weight of a sizeable truck. It could have taken a hundred years for this project to be completed. Three or four generations would have come and gone and the most they would have seen would have been a large store of stones somewhere on the plain.

This use of stones which have been brought many miles seems to be one of the characteristics of Neolithic monuments. The biggest stone still standing in Britain, for instance, is in Rudston churchyard, a few miles inland from Bridlington in Humberside. It stands high on the chalk wolds, but is itself made of gritstone, a rock found no nearer than ten miles away. At present it is over eight metres high above ground and its base is two metres across. Cutting it and dragging it ten miles uphill must have taken the effort of about 300 men and providing the leather ropes for the job would have taken the skins of dozens of cattle.

Similar feats of transportation would have been needed for the three Devil's Arrows at Boroughbridge in North Yorkshire and the single stone near the Goonhilly satellite-tracking station on the Lizard Peninsula, Cornwall. This latter stone is made of a type of granite found many miles away from where the stone stands. Equally mysterious is the block of stone near the churchyard at Shebbear in North Devon. Called the Devil's Stone, it is made of the same bluestone as the first ring at Stonehenge. Nobody knows for certain how it got there.

There are many megalithic monuments in the Presely region of Dyfed and it may well be that the bluestone from these hills was thought to have magical powers. Whatever the reason for taking the stones so far, the labourers involved in the project must have been keen volunteers. On a journey from Stonehenge to the

Rudston standing stone, All Saints Church, Rudston, North Humberside.

Presely mountains, which would have taken at least ten days, any unwilling stone-haulers could have escaped easily.

When the teams of workers arrived at the mountain with their supporting cooks and porters they would then face the difficult job of cutting the stone. They had no metal tools and so the blocks were removed from the rock face by splitting and chipping. Cracks may have been made by lighting fires along the grain of the rock and any splits produced could have been enlarged by hammering in wedges. The hot rock may also have been split by cooling it quickly with water. Slowly, and over a long period, they would make a block of the size needed. They would then have the problem of transporting it back to the henge on Salisbury Plain.

As the bluestones arrived other workers at the henge started to construct a double ring of upright stones inside the bank of the circle. It was a slow process and many years passed before the rings began to take shape. Then, for some reason, the plan was changed and the stones were removed. They now began the most advanced building project ever seen in Europe at this time. For the new structure they needed even bigger stones and so they used the large sandstone boulders on the Marlborough Downs. Compared with the bluestone extraction, the new project was very difficult. The Welsh stone was cut from the rock face; the Marlborough sandstone had to be dug from the ground. The bluestone blocks each weighed about 4 tonnes; the sandstone blocks in the new design each weighed up to 50 tonnes.

Dragging the new blocks on wooden sledges required ropes of enormous strength and it is thought that they used plaited leather strips which were long enough for as many as fifty men to pull. Each block would require several ropes at the front and the back to control the load on the hilly route from the downs to the henge. What is even more significant is the fact that hundreds of cattle would have to be killed and skinned to make the ropes. For a community struggling to find enough food to live on this was a remarkable sacrifice.

The new sandstone blocks were unique. They were smooth and rectangular in shape; all previous monuments had been made of rough-cut stone. The upright stones also had lintels across the top which were secured by mortice and tenon joints. An outer circle of stones was not only perfectly circular with an accuracy of ±8 cm, but its ring of lintels was also perfectly level. Each lintel was also slightly curved so that the overall effect was of a continuous ring of stone delicately poised in the air. Inside the circle there was an arrangement of high trilithons ('three stones', or two upright stones with a lintel across the top) forming a horseshoe.

Not only is the monument pleasing to the eye, it is also carefully arranged so that the stones and the gaps between stones are in line with the rising point of the sun and moon on the horizon on important days in the year. Stonehenge could, in fact, be used as a calendar to supply the farming community with information so that farmers would know when to plant their seeds. But it must have meant more than this because something far less elaborate would have provided the same information. The arrangement of the monument with the horseshoe's open end facing the rising midsummer sun suggests that it was built for some kind of ceremony. It looks like a temple.

The fifty-six holes of the original henge, called the Aubrey holes because they were first discovered by the seventeenth century archaeologist John Aubrey, may also be connected with the moon. We think this because of the irregular movements of the moon in relation to the earth. Like the sun, the moon rises in the east and sets in the west. This apparent movement is due to the rotation of the earth on its axis. (The moon is actually moving east when viewed against the background of the stars.) From time to time the light from the sun does not reach the moon because the earth is in between them. This is called an *eclipse* of the moon and it can be predicted because the movements of earth, sun and moon are very regular when observed over a long period of time. In fact, the moon's cycle of movements takes fifty-six years to complete. This means that there is a predictable pattern of eclipses which repeats itself every fifty-six years. If Stone Age men knew this, then the Aubrey holes could be year markers for the priests at Stonehenge. Each year something could be moved to the next hole and they would know whether a moon-eclipse was to be expected that year. On such days they could be ready to perform ceremonies to make sure that the moon did not disappear for ever.

Avebury
Stonehenge is the best-known circle, but in comparison with Avebury it is only moderate in size. Avebury has one big circle with two smaller ones inside it, but these inner circles are so big that fifteen Stonehenges would fit inside one of them. The big circle at Avebury is over 400 metres in diameter; Stonehenge is only 26 metres in diameter.

Avebury is also part of an even larger complex of monuments. Leading towards it from the south-east there is Kennet Avenue, a double row of tall stones more than a mile long which joins Avebury to another circle (now destroyed) called the Sanctuary. There are also traces of another double row of stones leading in the direction of the village of Beckhampton to the west. Between these two avenues and to the south is Silbury Hill which has been described in a previous chapter. Further south still, on the brow of a ridge, is West Kennet Long Barrow.

Prehistoric Geometry
The outer ring of Stonehenge is circular; Avebury's two inner rings are also circular, but the main ring is a strange shape made up of five intersecting arcs. This feature is similar to the shapes of other ancient rings. Accurate surveys have shown that the shapes of rings can be divided into four categories:

True circles	Egg-shaped rings
Flattened circles	Ellipses

Today, if a mathematics teacher asks you to draw an ellipse, you would need to use geometrical instruments. In the Stone Age they probably used a system of posts and loops of rope to mark out their massive shapes. The difficult part would be placing the blocks of stone exactly on the lines.

Solving mathematical problems can be an enjoyable experience and the Stone Age mathematicians probably got pleasure from working out new shapes and building them. An engineer and mathematician, Alexander Thom, has shown us how one of the rings can be drawn on paper. You might like to try to draw it yourself.

First, draw two adjacent right-angled triangles with sides 3, 4 and 5 cms long, having the 3 cm side in common.

AB = 4 cms   BD = 4 cms   BC = 3 cms   AC = 5 cms
CD = 5 cms

Extend the lines AD, AC and DC as shown in the diagram. Then with centre B describe a semi-circle radius 7 cms. With centre A describe an arc radius 11 cms. With centre D describe an arc radius 11 cms. With centre C describe an arc radius 6 cms. The arcs and semi-circle should flow into each other at the points where they intersect with the extended lines. This egg-shape is the ground-plan of the ring of stones called the Druid Temple, which is near Inverness. The actual ring has a main diameter of 15 metres.

The mathematical shapes and alignments with sun, moon and stars show us that the people of the New Stone Age were not ignorant savages. Their culture was different from ours, but it was surprisingly advanced. Their monuments, however, were more than mathematical laboratories or observatories. They were connected with their religious beliefs. All of them have burials nearby and most of them are suitable settings for religious ceremonies.

In other places than Britain people have been taking a close look at stone monuments. High in the Bighorn Mountains of Wyoming, for instance, there is a ring of stones about twenty-seven metres in diameter. Near to it there is a pile of stones and at the time of the midwinter solstice (shortest day) a person standing at the centre of the ring would see the sun rise exactly over the stones. There is a similar alignment at the Moose Mountain Medicine Wheel at Saskatchewan in Canada.

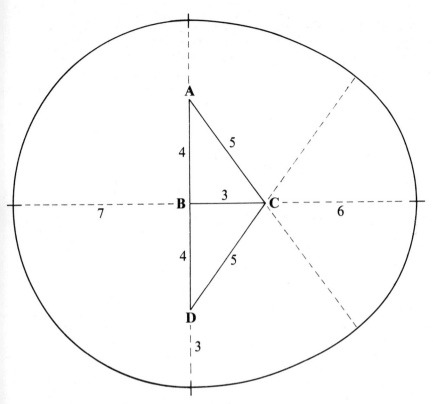

Plan of Druid Temple, Inverness showing geometrical construction.

Conclusion

Standing stones are impressive. Most of them are very heavy, and cutting and moving them would have been very difficult. What is even more surprising is the way they are arranged with great precision so that they line up with sun, moon and star positions. They also follow the lines of elaborate geometrical shapes in some cases. They seem to be connected with the worship of the sun, moon and stars, and may have been calendars, telling early man about the changes in the seasons, but this was probably a secondary function. For the people of those times the sun, moon and stars were gods upon whom they were dependent.

Any place where they thought a god was present or a god's power was experienced was sacred. Trees, springs and the banks of rivers were the settings for ceremonies which attempted to make sure that plant, animal and human life continued on earth.

Some of the ceremonies performed around the standing stones may have involved dancing men and women taking part, and this may be why many of them have folklore and legends concerning dancing maidens and wedding parties. Some of the bigger rings, like Avebury and Long Meg, would have been ideal settings for this kind of activity.

Revision Exercise

1 What do the following Celtic words mean: dolmen, men scryfa, men-an-tol, menhir?
2 How do we know that the Heel Stone at Stonehenge was connected with the sun?
3 In what way does Stonehenge differ from all other stone rings?
4 Why do we think that the stone rings were religious monuments and not just observatories?
5 Name the two places where the stones for Stonehenge came from.

Things to Do

1 Discuss with the rest of your class the reasons for building these rings of stone. Remember that there are about 600 of them in Britain.
2 Imagine that you are a member of the team sent to fetch the bluestones from Wales. Write a composition describing your experiences on the way.
3 Study an atlas of southern England and Wales and suggest the best route for bringing the stones to Salisbury Plain. Archaeologists think that the easiest route was probably along rivers with the stones floating on huge rafts.
4 Go out onto your school field and pace out one of the big rings to get some idea of its size. The outer ring is about 400 metres in diameter and had 100 stones.

For Further Study

'Religious Ritual', *Encyclopaedia Britannica* Macropaedia, Vol. 18, pp. 218–9.
BURL, A. (1976) *Stone Circles of the British Isles* Yale University Press
ATKINSON, R.J.C. (1959) *Stonehenge and Avebury and Neighbouring Monuments* HMSO

5 Clues in Literature

The study of early religion is difficult because there are few written records. Nothing was written down in Britain in the Old and New Stone Ages, and, even as late as 1300 BC, the only people who could write lived in the Near East. For this reason we turn to the Bible as a source of ancient beliefs in the hope that it will throw some light on the beliefs of those who lived at the same time as the biblical writers but could not write. In doing this, however, we must remember that we cannot be certain that a standing stone in Canaan was put there for the same reason as a standing stone in Britain.

We shall also refer to other ancient books, some of which may be in your school library. These again may not be entirely reliable because they were written in many cases by those who opposed the religions they are describing. Nevertheless we have to use them because they are amongst the only records we have and they do offer us clues to the beliefs of others. It is the task of the student of history to compare one account with another and to look for one-sided or exaggerated accounts.

To simplify the search for clues we are going to look for information on three areas of interest: (1) Ancient beliefs regarding the sun, moon and stars; (2) Ancient beliefs concerning standing stones; (3) Ancient beliefs concerning trees.

1 Sun, Moon and Stars

The Jews believed in one God and the Old Testament emphasizes that this one God created all things, including the sun, moon and stars. Some of the people living in neighbouring countries thought that the sun, moon and stars were gods, and so the Bible often contrasts the one God of Israel with the gods of the heathen neighbours.

Great is the Lord . . .
For all the gods of the people are idols; but the Lord made the heavens.

1 Chronicles 16:26–27

When the Bible speaks of 'the heavens', it means all the objects in the sky above us. On dark nights, ancient men and women spent many hours gazing into the sky and wondering. One biblical poet expresses his thoughts in the following words:

When I look at the heavens, the work of thy fingers,
the moon and the stars which thou hast established;
What is man that thou art mindful of him?

Psalm 8:3–4

Today most of us would find it difficult to distinguish between the constellations in the night-sky, but in ancient times there were those who could identify them and follow their movements. The prophet Amos (*c.* 750 BC), for instance, knew about the constellations of Pleiades and Orion (Amos 5: 8), and may have used their movements to determine the time of year.

Centuries earlier, the Babylonians referred to their interest in the constellations in the *Epic of Creation* which was chanted at the New Year Festival. The Epic dates from about 1000 BC and describes the victory of the god Marduk over a chaos-monster. In the fourth tablet we read:

He constructed stations for the great gods,
Fixing their astral likenesses in the constellations . . .
He set up three constellations for each of the twelve months . .

The ideas of the Babylonians and of other neighbours of Israel at different times influenced the religious beliefs and practices of the Jews and in spite of the warnings of prophets they occasionally lapsed into worship of the sun, moon and stars. The warnings of the prophets are sternly proclaimed in the following words:

If there is found among you a man or a woman who does what is wrong . . . and has gone to serve other gods and worshipped them, or the sun, or the moon or any of the hosts of heaven . . . You shall stone that man or woman to death.

Deuteronomy 17:2–5

Just as there were lapses, so there were periods of reform when someone took action to put things right. One such reformer was

King Josiah, who reigned in the seventh century BC, the time of Celtic influence in Europe. Here is what he did:

> He deposed the priests ordained to burn incense in the high places . . . those who burned incense to Baal, to the sun, and the moon and the constellations . . .

2 Kings 23:5

Judaism still has interesting ceremonies connected with the sun and moon. The new month is blessed during a ceremony called *Rosh Hodesh* (the Hebrew word *hodesh* means moon or month). As the new moon is not visible for three days, Jews wait until the new crescent can be seen and then say special prayers and read portions of the Law of Moses, including:

> At the beginning of your moons you shall offer a burnt offering to the Lord: two young bulls, one ram, seven male lambs a year old without blemish; also three tenths of an ephah of fine flour . . .

Numbers 28:11–12

The ceremony is performed in the open air and also includes the ritual of standing on tiptoes three times. At one time people would dance.

There is also a ceremony for the blessing of the sun which takes place every twenty-eight years during the Hebrew month of Nisan. On this day it was believed that the sun was in the position in the sky which it occupied when God created the world. It last occurred on Wednesday (the fourth day of creation, Genesis 1:14), April 8th, 1981, and on that day Jews throughout the world got up at sunrise to bless the sun. They included a small group on the top of the Empire State Building in New York City.

The Christian festival of Easter is also connected with the sun and moon. Like the Jewish Passover, it is determined by the date of the first full moon after the Spring Equinox. This is why the date of Easter varies from year to year. If the first full moon comes soon after the Spring Equinox then Easter is early. Christmas also falls on an important sun-day: the former midwinter solstice, or shortest day. Nowadays, of course, the midwinter solstice happens a few days before Christmas Day.

To find Easter today, we simply have to consult a calendar, but in the early days of Christianity there were no calendars. This is why astronomy was important even before the telescope had been invented. In a book called *A History of the English Church and People*, for instance, written about 1200 years ago by a British monk, we are told that a good education consisted of the study of the Bible, poetry, astronomy, and the calculation of the Church's calendar.

Towards the end of the book, there is a letter from an abbot called Ceolfrid to the King of the Picts, in which he explains about the full moon of the Passover and the Spring Equinox. He tells the King that the moon goes round the earth along a slightly different orbit each year for nineteen years, and after that 'all that concerns the sequences of sun and moon, month and week, recurs in the same order as before'. This nineteen-year cycle is sometimes called the Metonic Cycle, after the Greek astronomer who wrote about it in the fifth century BC. It has been suggested that some of the stone rings with nineteen standing stones, such as Rosemodress Circle at Boleigh in Cornwall, were built by people who knew about this nineteen-year cycle.

Another important old book which shows what an interest there was in astronomy in ancient times is the *Anglo-Saxon Chronicle*. Throughout the book there are references to the sun, moon and stars. Here are some examples:

In the year 1104 the first day of Whitsuntide was on the 5th of June, and on the following Tuesday at noon there appeared four intersecting halos around the sun, white in colour, and looking as if they had been painted. All who saw it were astonished . . .

In the year 793 terrible portents appeared over Northumbria, and miserably frightened the inhabitants: these were exceptional flashes of lightning, and fiery dragons were seen flying in the air . . .

In the year 975 Edward succeeded to the throne: and soon in the autumn of the same year appeared that star known as 'comet'.

802: In this year there was an eclipse of the moon at dawn on the 20th December.

In our world of electric lights and central heating we do not spend much time looking at the night-sky. In ancient times, however, the sky was where gods and spirits lived, and so men and women were always looking at it for signs. They knew that they depended on the sun for life, and the sun, moon and stars seemed to control the seasons. It was important, therefore, to keep an eye on what these gods were doing. Any unusual events were taken as warnings.

It is useful for us to note that old religions like Judaism still have ceremonies connected with the sun and moon and that one of them takes place only every twenty-eight years. Although there might not have been any link between the Stone Age communities in Britain and those living in the Near East, they probably had some points of view in common. The builders of the megalithic monuments may also have had sun and moon ceremonies, some of which took place only every nineteen, twenty-eight or fifty-six years.

2 Standing Stones

Many primitive cultures have monuments made from massive pieces of rock. They are found in ancient America, Africa and India, as well as Europe. The Old Testament has several references to them and it seems fairly certain that when the Israelites entered Canaan about 1250 BC sacred stones were of three types:

1 Single standing stones
2 Standing stones near to wooden poles
3 Groups of stones

The prophets of Israel repeatedly warned the people not to follow the ways of their heathen neighbours, but it is obvious that stones were sometimes used by them in their worship.

The first reference to a standing stone is found in the story of Jacob, told in Genesis. One night he was on a long journey and he rested and had a dream. In his dream he saw a ladder stretching up to heaven with angels ascending and descending. God then appeared above the ladder and promised Jacob that he would have many descendants. In the morning 'he took the stone which he had put under his head and set it up for a pillar and poured oil on top of it' (Genesis 28:18). He called the place Bethel, a Hebrew word meaning 'house of God'. This incident

43

may offer an important clue to the purpose of other standing stones. Do they also mark the place where someone had a deeply-moving religious experience or a dream?

Later on in the story of Jacob we are told how he buried his wife Rachel and marked her grave with a stone pillar (Genesis 35:20). It must have been a stone of some size because it was still standing when this part of the book of Genesis was written.

Some years later when the Israelites entered Canaan under the leadership of Joshua they came under the influence of Canaanite religion. Even when they were remembering their agreement to remain faithful to the God of Israel, Joshua 'took a great stone, and set it up there under the oak in the sanctuary of the Lord' (Joshua 24:26). This combination of standing stone and sacred tree was typical of the Canaanites.

Arrangements of standing stones are also mentioned in the Old Testament. After receiving the Ten Commandments, for instance, Moses built a stone altar and then set up twelve stone pillars (Exodus 24:4). We are not told how the stones were arranged, but a circular setting is possible. On another occasion, the Israelites set up twelve pillars to commemorate a miraculous crossing of the River Jordan. In this case the stones cannot have been very large because they carried them on their shoulders. On the other hand, they must have been conspicuous because they were set up as a memorial for all time (Joshua 4:5–7).

3 Trees

Oak trees were sacred to the Canaanites and to many other people since. So too were wooden poles which they called *asherim*. They were symbols of the goddess Astarte, who was also called the Queen of Heaven. The Law of Moses condemned these poles, but the Israelites often used them. During the reign of King Rehoboam, for instance, many Canaanite customs were followed:

> Judah did what was evil in the sight of the Lord . . . for they built for themselves high places, and pillars, and Asherim on every high hill and under every green tree; and there were also male cult prostitutes in the land

1 Kings 14:22–23

Here again we may have a valuable clue to the religion of prehistoric societies in Britain. Archaeologists have found holes in

44

Left, a sixteenth century maypole; *right*, Astarte, gold pendant from Ugarit, fourteenth/fifteenth century BC.

which wooden posts once stood near to standing stones and stone rings. The wood has rotted away, but the shape of the holes is clear. It is possible that some of these poles were the British equivalent of *asherim.*

The reference to 'cult prostitutes' is interesting. It shows that sexual intercourse was a part of the religious ceremonies performed at these holy places. This is one of the reasons why the Old Testament prophets spoke out so strongly against this kind of religion.

Maypoles were condemned in Britain at one time for a similar reason. In the seventeenth century, for instance, a puritan called Thomas Hall said that he thought the May Day dances at the maypole were wrong:

If Moses were angry when he saw the people dance about a golden calf, well may he be angry to see people dancing the morrice about a post in honour of a whore.

45

The 'morrice' he refers to was a dance similar to the Morris dances we see today. The 'whore' was the May Queen. She was the Medieval equivalent of the goddess Astarte, and her pole was similar to the *asherim*.

Yew trees were also important in early religion and they were planted in ancient churchyards to repel evil forces. Sometimes yew trees live for more than a thousand years and they may be older than the building they stand near to.

Conclusion

From the very earliest of times men and women have seen a connection between the movements of the sun, moon and stars and the seasons of the year. They did not understand how the weather got warmer at certain times of the year and colder at others and how this affected the growth of crops. The fertility of animals was also a mystery to them. They only knew that the regular cycles of events in the sky seemed to influence the cycle of events on earth. They planned their ceremonies so that they would please the sky gods. In the ancient world these ceremonies were an attempt to make sure that plant, animal and human life continued on earth.

Revision Exercise

1 Why were ancient peoples so interested in the movements of sun, moon and stars?
2 What sort of things did King Josiah do in his reforms?
3 Why does the date of Passover and Easter vary from year to year?
4 What is Rosh Hodesh?
5 What happened to Jacob at Bethel?

Things to Do

1 Find out what causes an eclipse of the sun, an eclipse of the moon and the tides.
2 Why do we always see the same face of the moon? Why does the moon appear the same size as the sun from the earth? See if you can find the answers to these questions.
3 Make a list of songs and poems about the moon. Compile an anthology.
4 Ask your parents and grandparents about superstitions concerning the sun, moon and stars.

Passages in the Bible for Further Study

The Old Testament was written in Hebrew and sometimes we use one English word to translate several Hebrew words. In the lists below there are the places in the Bible where you can find the Hebrew words for 'trees' and 'stones'. If you read the passages carefully and compare them with one another, you will build up a picture of the part played by stones and trees in the Jewish religion.

matstebah, 'pillar of stone'
Genesis 28:18, 22; 31:13, 45, 51, 52; 35:14, 20
Exodus 23:24; 24:4; 34:13
Leviticus 26:1
Deuteronomy 12:3; 16:22
1 Kings 14:23
2 Kings 17:10
2 Samuel 18:18
Isaiah 19:19
Jeremiah 43:13
Hosea 3:4
Micah 5:13

eben, 'stone'
Joshua 4:3; 7:26; 8:29; 24:26
1 Samuel 6:14
2 Samuel 18:17

asherah, 'grove of trees'
Exodus 34:13
Deuteronomy 16:21
Judges 3:7; 6:26
2 Kings 17:9–12
2 Chronicles 33:1–6

elah, 'oak'
Ezekiel 6:13

allon, 'oak'
Hosea 4:13

elim, 'oak'
Isaiah 1:29; see also Isaiah 65:3–4

6 Celts and Anglo-Saxons

In about 2000 BC men and women in Britain began to use copper and other metals with low melting points. They were not very suitable for tools because they were soft, although bronze (a mixture of copper and tin) was hard and tools made of bronze had a good cutting edge. A thousand years later they were able to heat up furnaces to much higher temperatures and extract iron from ore. Although iron rusts easily, it is very good for tools and weapons because it is hard and can be sharpened to a fine edge.

Groups of iron-working people, or Celts, came to Britain from the continent between about 800 BC and the coming of the Romans in AD 43. They built the hill-forts which are scattered all over the country, and gave us coinage for trade and the potter's wheel.

The hill-forts were surrounded by banks and ditches. We can tell by the remaining banks that they were often high and would have had strong fences along the top. The ditches had steep sides and were on the outside of the bank. Any invaders would have to go down into the ditch before scaling the bank and would have been easy targets for the fort's defenders.

One fort, called Maiden Castle, near Dorchester in Dorset, was so well fortified with four massive banks and ditches, that it took the Roman Second Legion under a general called Vespasian to conquer it. The Romans were successful because they were armed with deadly ballista-arrows. They could fire accurately at the British without getting too close.

The Celts also cut enormous figures in the turf on the steep slopes of the chalk downland of southern Britain. One of the best-known is the figure of a man with outstretched arms, each of which is holding a long pole. It is at Wilmington in East Sussex and is eighty metres tall. Another is the strange long horse with a forked tongue at Uffington in Oxfordshire. It is over a hundred metres long from head to tail. The most unusual of all is the sixty-metre Cerne Giant, a naked man holding a large club, on the steep slope above the parish church of Cerne Abbas.

All the figures can be seen from the valley below and the surrounding hills, but are most clearly seen from above. This suggests they were put there for the benefit of the gods in the sky.

Above, aerial view of Maiden Castle, Dorset; *below*, the Long Man, Wilmington, East Sussex.

Druids

The Celtic priests were called druids. We know little about them because they passed on information about their beliefs and customs by word of mouth. As far as we know, they did not write anything down. Some information can be found in books written by Romans, but we have to take care because Celts and Romans were enemies and what has been written may be one-sided or exaggerated.

Druid temples were often made of wood, although they sometimes made stone buildings. They were small and it is their natural setting which was important. They were built on hill-tops, near clumps of trees, by rivers and by springs. Abandoned megalithic monuments may also have been used by them.

The word 'druid' probably comes from the Greek word *drus*, which means 'oak tree'. The second part of the word may come from *wid*, which means 'to know'. Both parts of the word point to important aspects of the Celtic religion. It was a nature religion with an interest in trees, and the priests of the religion claimed to have special knowledge. They knew about life after death and they knew about the movements of the sun, moon and stars. Their gods are not easy to identify, but it does seem clear that they worshipped animals, fish and birds.

Sacred Groves

Groves are small woods or groups of trees. In Celtic times they were often holy places and were used for religious ceremonies. A Roman poet of the first century called Lucan wrote a description of a sacred grove near Marseilles:

> A grove . . . whose interlacing boughs enclosed a space of darkness and cold shade . . . Gods were worshipped there with savage rites, the altars were heaped with hideous offerings, and every tree was sprinkled with human gore . . . The images of the gods, grim and rude, were uncouth blocks, formed of felled tree-trunks . . .

The place was so evil, he tells us, that birds and animals would not go near it. Even though we do not know how much he might have exaggerated this description, it does seem clear that the druids offered sacrifices and used human blood in their worship.

Many people feel uneasy in a dark wood and in some country areas there are woods where local people will not go. There seems to be something uncanny and mysterious about such places and they sometimes cause us to shudder. In spite of this they still fascinate us. This may be one of the reasons why the druids chose them for their ceremonies.

The Celtic word *nemeton* means 'sacred grove' or 'sacred place in a woodland clearing'. Quite a number of English place-names derived from the word. Just north of Dartmoor, for instance, there is an area which must have been very important to the Celts. The River Nymet starts near the village of South Tawton and as it flows northwards it passes several villages with names which include part of the word *nemeton*. It is also interesting to note that six miles from its source it passes Oak Tree Farm. The church of South Tawton, which may have stood on the site of a pagan temple, has a remarkable collection of wood-carvings on the bosses in the roof. They include several strange heads peering from leaves and with leaves growing out of their mouths. They were put there in the Middle Ages and represent the gods or demons which lived in the woods. The fact that there are so many in this church suggests a strong belief in sacred groves even when Christianity had replaced the pagan beliefs.

Hill-tops

Hills which were imposing or isolated were chosen for temples. If you visit one of these places today you can see why. The views are usually exhilarating and a person standing there feels small in comparison with everything else. The sky is big, the stars seem nearer. Man probably felt closer to his gods in such places.

The Celts loved the hills and they lived on the hill-tops. When the Romans came, they conquered the hill-forts and then made their towns and built their villas in the valleys below. A Celtic poem from Medieval Ireland called *The Hill of Howth* gives us an indication of their attitude:

Delightful to be on the Hill of Howth . . .
The peak bright-knolled beyond all hills,
with its hill-top round and green and rugged . . .
The peak that is loveliest throughout the land of Ireland,
the bright peak above the sea of gulls, it is a hard step for me
to leave it, lovely hill of delightful Howth.

The word *pen* may be Celtic for 'hill'. It is used in connection with hills, for example, in Penyghent, the Pennine summit, and

Pendle Hill, the famous Lancashire hill. Some of these hills were sanctuaries. Pilsdon Pen, marked on the map as a hill-fort, was probably a Celtic temple. It is the highest point in Dorset and from its summit can be seen six hill-forts within a radius of fifteen miles. One can imagine these early Britons coming from all directions to gather on Pilsdon Pen for religious festivals.

Celtic Festivals

Samhain was the first day of the Celtic year. It fell on November 1st in our calendar and was the day when the living could make contact with the dead. We still remember it today when we celebrate Hallowe'en the evening before. Nowadays, of course, few people take the idea of ghosts seriously, but for the Celts it was an important day. When Christianity came to Britain, the Samhain festival was changed to All Saints Day (November 1st) and All Souls Day (November 2nd).

The second major festival was *Imbolc* which was celebrated on February 1st. It was connected with fertility and was transformed into the festival of Saint Brigid or Bride by the Celtic church. She is said to have lived in Ireland around AD 500.

Beltain was celebrated on May 1st and it marked a division between the cold half and hot half of the year. This was the time when the sun was beginning to gain strength and get hotter and so fires were lit on the tops of hills. People and cattle would walk around the blazing fires.

The last festival of the year was *Lugnasadh* (August 1st). It seems to have been connected with cattle and crops. The Christian festival of Lammas (loaf-mass) seems to have replaced it as a harvest festival.

It is interesting to note that the four Celtic festivals are not on important days in the astronomical calendar, such as midsummer's day or midwinter's day. They are important days in the farmer's calendar. Christianity made holy days out of these Celtic festivals and out of the major sun festivals as well.

Rivers and Lakes

When the runway was being extended at R.A.F. Valley on Anglesey in 1943, a bulldozer unearthed a large collection of objects from the Celtic period. They included bronze bridle bits, chains, swords and spear-heads. They were in the mud of what had previously been part of a small lake called Llyn Cerrig Bach near the north-west corner of the island. It soon became clear that these had been offerings to the gods which had been thrown into the lake. Similar collections of valuable objects have been found in other lakes.

Rivers were also sacred and precious objects were often thrown into them as offerings to the gods. In the British Museum there is a beautiful shield dating from about the time of the birth of Christ which was found in the Thames at Battersea. It was most probably an offering to the river-goddess. Some rivers are named after goddesses. Brent and Braint, for example, come from Brigantia; Severn comes from Sabrina. The sources of rivers were also important and many Celtic holy springs were converted into holy wells by the Christian Church. The custom of throwing money into wishing wells is the modern equivalent of making an offering to the river-goddess.

Animals
Animals and birds were sacred to the Celts. The horse, for instance, is found carved in the chalk on hills in a number of places in southern England. It may represent Epona, the horse-goddess. The traditional rhyme: 'Good luck to you, good luck to me, good luck to every white horse I see', may have come to us from a time when white horses were thought to bring a blessing to the people. As chalk figures are usually near to hill-forts, they may have been put there by the inhabitants for protection.

Horses often play a part in Morris dances and other May Day rituals. At Padstow in Cornwall and Minehead in Somerset there are ceremonies involving hobby horses which are connected with the coming of Spring. The Padstow horse has also been seen as a giver of fertility and at one time women who were to be married would stoop under the skirt of the horse to make sure that they would have children.

The horns of animals were also important, particularly those of the deer. There seems to have been a fascination with the antlers of deer. After the animals had dropped them in the springtime they would be collected so that they could be used as tools. They were harder than any other material used by the Celts apart from stone and were a suitable shape. The strength of antlers and their rapid growth led people to think that the strength of the animals was concentrated there.

At Abbots Bromley in Staffordshire there is a ceremony each September which shows some of these early beliefs. At daybreak on a Monday morning six men dress up in Medieval costume.

Obby Oss ritual, Padstow, Cornwall.

Antler ritual, Abbots Bromley, Staffordshire.

Three are in black and three in white. They go to the parish church and collect six sets of stag antlers which are kept in the church. Then, accompanied by a hobby horse, they walk through the village. The two colours represent summer and winter and the ceremony is an attempt to make certain that the summer will return again after the winter. It is as if they are wanting the mysterious forces which are concentrated in the antlers to work for them.

Other animals considered divine included the bull, dog, cat, boar, ram and goat. Some of them are still associated with the

54

old religion. Cats, for example, especially black ones, are often connected with witches who were important in paganism. Today we tend to look on witches with amusement, but in the past they were the men and women who had a mysterious knowledge of life, health and death. The name 'witch' comes from *wicca*, which means 'to know'. They knew how to call on supernatural forces and they tried to use this power for good and for evil. In a similar way, goats are connected with the devil: often in old engravings and wood-carvings the devil is shown in the form of a goat.

Salmon and trout were also thought to be gods. One reason for this was the amazing way these fish could make their way up shallow and fast flowing streams. As if by magic they appeared in pools near sacred springs. Today, trout can be found in a number of what were Celtic holy places. At Little Bredy, for instance, there are many trout in a large pool called Bridehead. The pool is fed by several small streams which rise in the Valley of Stones, so called because of the large number of sandstone boulders scattered along its bottom. Some of the boulders have been arranged in circles and on the hills above the valley there are several Stone Age monuments made from the stones. The river flowing from the pool is the Bredy, a name derived from the Celtic word *Bride*, the name of a goddess. Just above the pool is the Church of Saint Michael, a confirmation that the site was a pagan sanctuary because Christians dedicated churches built on pagan holy places to the angel Michael.

The Cult of the Head and Human Sacrifice
The Celts thought that the human head had magical powers. Some of their temples were decorated with the heads of enemies or sacrificial victims. These heads either stood in niches around the walls or else were suspended from hooks. In some cases heads were carved in stone. The frequent use of heads in the decoration of early Christian churches shows us that superstition about the head took a long time to disappear.

Perhaps the most gruesome Celtic ceremony was that involving a giant wicker figure. According to Roman writers the druids built a giant figure of a man out of long twigs taken from trees like the willow. Its legs were fat enough to take a human body. When the colossus was finished, it was filled with living bodies and then burnt.

Human sacrifice has been practised by several religions, but it is not easy to see why it was done. When Abraham was asked to

Left, Celtic stone head, Corbridge, Northumberland; *right*, Gundestrup silver cauldron, first century BC, showing tribal gods, animals and hunters.

offer his son Isaac as a burnt offering on a hill-top in the land of Morah, we are told that it was to test Abraham's faith (Genesis 22:2, 12). Centuries later, king Ahaz of Judah burned his son as an offering when he was influenced by the religion of the Canaanites (2 Kings 16:3). Throughout the Bible, however, human sacrifice is condemned.

The Aztecs of Mexico were in favour of human sacrifice and from what is known of them it seems that it was meant to feed the gods. They thought that the gods must be strong if they were to bless the people and so they kept them supplied with human blood. The archaeological evidence is horrific and the records of the Spanish who conquered the Aztecs tell a grisly tale. At the dedication of the extensions to a temple, for instance, 20,000 people were sacrificed – the population of a small town. In comparison with this the Celtic religion does not seem so bad.

Saxons and Vikings

When the Celts had been in Britain for over 500 years the Romans sent two expeditions led by Julius Caesar. Almost a hundred years later in AD 43 the emperor Claudius sent an army which succeeded in conquering the Celtic tribes. Britain became part of the Roman Empire.

The Romans brought their own gods and temples and the religious life of the Britons was influenced by them. The Celtic traditions remained, however, in Ireland, Wales, Scotland and Cornwall – the areas more or less untouched by the Romans.

During the Roman occupation, Christianity became the official religion of the empire, but for the majority of people the old religions remained strong.

The Roman occupation ended soon after AD 400 when the legions had to return to defend the city of Rome itself. This left Britain almost defenceless and so Jutes, Angles and Saxons, who had previously been content with coastal raids, now began to settle here. They brought with them new forms of paganism, and although they soon turned to Christianity, their paganism left its mark on our culture and traditions. Much of what we know about the religion of the Anglo-Saxons has come to us from Bede, a monk who lived in Northumberland about AD 700.

Bede tells us that the Anglo-Saxon year had ten months, although two of the months were twice as long as the others. It began on December 25th with the first month called Yule. The fourth month also has an interesting name – *Eostre* – from which we get Easter. The eleventh month was called *Blotmonath*, 'Bloodmonth', and was the time when most of the cattle which could not be fed during the winter were slaughtered. The killing was seen as a massive offering to the gods.

We have only a vague idea about their gods. The important ones seem to have been Woden, Tiw, Thor and Frig. Woden, or Odin as he is sometimes called, was the father of gods. His wife was Frig, and she was a goddess of fertility. Some of these names are incorporated in English place-names. Tysoe in Warwickshire, for example, was probably named after Tiw, the war-god. The Anglo-Saxons defeated their enemies there in the Vale of the Red Horse.

Vikings began their attacks on Britain about AD 900 and they too brought their gods with them. Like the Saxon gods they are difficult to identify. Odin was the chief god and Viking warriors looked forward to the day when heavenly maidens would take them to feast with him in a large hall called Valhalla. The heavenly maidens are called Valkyries and Valhalla was thought to be part of the land of the gods which was called Asgard.

Conclusion

After the Stone Age several new religions were introduced to Britain by settlers from the continent. The Celts came and their influence still remains today. They did not build many temples, but their sanctuaries were in natural settings: in woods, on hills and by water.

The Romans brought their beliefs, built their temples and then went away again. Though the names were different, the Roman gods were similar to those of the Celts, and the one influenced the other. Christianity came to Britain during the Roman period and took root amongst the Celts, but the old religion persisted.

Anglo-Saxons and Vikings brought a different religious insight to Britain, but they too soon accepted Christianity, although the old and new religions intermingled for many centuries.

Revision Exercise
1 Who were the druids and what does their name mean?
2 Name three types of places where the Celts built their sanctuaries.
3 What happened at the Celtic feast called Beltain?
4 Give one reason why some religions practise human sacrifice.
5 What interesting facts do we learn about the Anglo-Saxon calendar from Bede? Do they tell us anything about the influence of paganism on our traditions?

Things to Do
1 Look on an Ordnance Survey map to see if there are any hill-forts near to you. Try to arrange a visit to one of them.
2 Study local place-names and river names to see whether any of them are connected with pagan gods. A good book to use is the *Oxford Dictionary of English Place-Names.*
3 Find out what you can about May Day traditions. If possible, arrange for a Morris dancer to come and explain about the origin and meaning of the dances.
4 Find out more about the druids and their activities at Stonehenge on Midsummer's Day.
5 Study the following passages in the Old Testament and see what similarities there are between the religion of the Canaanites and the religion of the Celts: 2 Kings 16:3; 17:17; 21:6; Deuteronomy 12:29–31.

Encyclopaedia Britannica, **Articles for Further Study**
'Brigit', Micropaedia, Vol. II, p. 271
'Celtic Religion', Micropaedia, Vol. II, p. 675
'Celtic Religion', Macropaedia, Vol. 3, p. 1068–1071
'Danu, Anu' (Earth Mother), Micropaedia, Vol. III, p. 374
'Druids', Micropaedia, Vol. III, p. 674

7 Christianity and the Old Religion

We know that there were Christians in Britain during the time of the Roman occupation because of Christian inscriptions and mosaics from the period. A villa in Dorset, for instance, had a mosaic floor with the two Greek letters *chi* and *rho* at its centre. These are the first two letters of 'Christ' in Greek and were used by Christians as a sign of their faith from an early date. This floor can now be seen at the British Museum.

Missionaries came over from Gaul, and soldiers and traders who were Christians also brought their faith to the native British. By the second century there were Christians here who were willing to die for their beliefs. Alban, for example, who lived in the Roman town of Verulamium, was beheaded because he was a Christian in the year AD 209. Saint Albans is the present name of Verulamium.

By AD 314 the Church in Britain was large enough to send a delegation to a meeting of Christian leaders at Arles in Gaul. Less than a hundred years later, a British monk called Pelagius was so confident about his own understanding of the New Testament that he attacked the views of Augustine, one of the leaders of the Catholic Church.

Patrick was also an important British Christian leader living at the same time as Pelagius. As a boy he was taken to Ireland by pirates, but he escaped six years later and returned to Britain where he trained as a priest. In AD 432 he went back to Ireland to preach the gospel.

In AD 597 a group of missionaries from Rome under the leadership of another man called Augustine landed in Kent. By this time the Celtic Church here had been developing independently of the Church in southern Europe to such an extent that some of its beliefs and customs were not the same as those of the Catholics. In 664 the two churches met at Whitby and sorted out their differences.

In spite of this activity on the part of Christian missionaries, there were still large areas where paganism flourished. Also, as most of the people could not read or write, their grasp of the Christian faith must have been very limited. For many of them,

Jesus was probably just another god to add to those already worshipped. Pagan temples were still used well into the Christian period, and sometimes Christian churches reverted to the old religion. We can see the grip the old gods had on the popular mind in the way the calendar never changed. In the USSR the word for 'Sunday' means 'resurrection'; in Britain we still call it the day of the Sun-god.

Monday: day of the moon
Tuesday: day of Tiw, god of war
Wednesday: Woden's day
Thursday: Thor's day, god of thunder
Friday: Freya's or Frig's day
Saturday: Saturn's day

Conversion of Pagan Sites
The Christians needed churches for their services. To save time and expense the missionaries were told to use pagan temples after they had destroyed the idols. The early Christian writer, Bede, has preserved a copy of a letter sent to Abbot Mellitus by Pope Gregory which says:

If these temples are well-built, they must be purified from the worship of demons and dedicated to the service of the true God. In this way, we hope that the people, seeing that their temples are not destroyed, may abandon their error and, flocking more readily to their accustomed resorts, may come to know and adore the true God.

Gregory also points out that since the pagans held spectacular ceremonies, such as the sacrificing of oxen, they must be allowed to kill them at the time of Christian festivals – but this time not to the devil, but merely for a good feast. They were also to be allowed to build shelters out of branches around the church. This may have been the Christianizing of some of the Celtic rituals which were performed in sacred groves.

In some cases the changes did not last very long. Bede tells us that King Earpwald of the East Angles decided to become a Christian. Not long afterwards, however, his wife tried to persuade him to return to the old religion. He tried to combine both:

He tried to serve both Christ and the ancient gods, and had in the same temple an altar for the holy sacrifice of Christ side by side with an altar on which victims were offered to devils.

The victims were presumably animals.

Standing stones created a problem for the missionaries. They did not have the skill or enthusiasm of the Neolithic men who put them up, and so could not easily move them. Instead, they converted many of them into crosses. The massive stone at Rudston in North Humberside, for instance, was used as a cross, as its name shows. (The name 'rud' or 'rood' means 'a cross'.) The top part of the cross has now fallen, but its eight metre stump stands next to the church.

Some of the Celtic crosses in Britain may be converted standing stones. Cornish crosses often have feebly-carved figures on them and a rounded top. The position of the crosses sometimes betrays their Neolithic origin. There are two crosses, for example, near to the Rosemodress Circle at Boleigh which are accurately aligned with the centre of the circle. Two other standing stones on the other side of the circle are also aligned with the centre. Similar round-headed crosses are found in Scotland and Ireland. A few miles west of Ballygawley in County Tyrone, for instance, there is a cross with a solid ringhead on a hill-top near to the remains of a church. As the hill-top was a pre-Christian sanctuary, the cross was probably once a standing stone.

Several stones have a curious shouldered-shape. They are very similar to the megalithic pillars on Corsica which date from the New Stone Age. It has been suggested that they are phallic stones. If this is true, it did not prevent the church from naming them after saints, as in the case of Saint Piran's Cross near Perranporth in Cornwall.

Some communities made their feelings about the stones very clear. At Awliscombe in Devon, for example, there is a door-step made from a large roughly-cut standing stone. As the congregation entered the west door of Saint Michael's church they showed their contempt for the pagan stone by walking on it.

Some pagan sites were converted by building a church on top of them. Several churches are built on round barrows. When the church at Fimber in North Humberside was being restored a century ago, they found a Bronze Age body in a crouch-position with a food pot at the centre of a round barrow. The ancient church's foundations had been built exactly over the mound.

Right, St Piran's Cross, Penhale Sands, Cornwall; *below*, ruined church at centre of Neolithic henge, Knowlton, Dorset.

An especially interesting converted pagan site is at Knowlton in Dorset where an ancient church stands at the centre of a Neolithic henge. The church is now a ruin, having lasted only a few hundred years; the henge, still quite well-preserved, lasted over four thousand years. It is particularly interesting because local clergy have to mount a guard on the ruin at the time of Hallowe'en to prevent it being used by neopagans for witchcraft. The old religion still survives in the twentieth century.

Holy Water

Early Christian missionaries knew the powerful religious hold which wells and springs had on the people, and so many of these were Christianized. One way of doing this was to build a baptistery near to the spring or well. At Madron in Cornwall, the ruined Celtic Baptistery is a few metres away from the pagan spring called Madron Well. It is a building without a roof and is rarely used today. The spring, however, is still visited by people who throw in money, and next to it is a tree which is partly covered with strips of rag and tissue tied to its branches. These are *clooties*, put there so that the person represented by them will have good luck.

The odd location of some of Britain's cathedrals can be explained when we take into account the fact that they were built on or near pagan springs. Winchester Cathedral, for instance, once the largest building in the world, is built over running water. Each winter the crypt has to be closed because the water rises above the floor level. Fifty years ago, when the east end of the building began to sink because of subsidence in the foundations, a deep-sea diver had to be employed to put in new foundations. For several years he worked in the cold waters under the cathedral to secure the building. William Walker is remembered today by a small bronze statue of him in his diving-suit.

The names of some wells may reflect their pagan origin. Those dedicated to Saint Brigid and Saint Ann, for instance, may bear the Christianized form of the names of two Celtic goddesses, Bride and Anu.

Green Men

The representations of foliate heads in churches is particularly interesting. These strange heads, with branches and leaves growing out of the mouths, ears and nostrils, are more than mere decorations. There must have been some general agreement about their significance as they are so common and similar. It is also clear that they were gradually given a less prominent place in churches as the time went by. In early Norman churches, they are often at eye-level; in fifteenth century churches, they are usually high up in the building, almost out of sight.

Green Men are usually found in one of three places in an old church: on pillar capitals, on bench-ends, and on bosses. Occasionally they are found on corbels. In early Norman churches the heads are simple and the vegetation grows out of the

Green Man on bench-end, Church of the
Holy Ghost, Crowcombe, Somerset.

mouth. By the fifteenth and sixteenth centuries the heads often
take on a frightening appearance and foliage comes from nose
and ears as well. The leaves are often recognizable as oak or
hawthorn and acorns are sometimes included in the carving.

We do not know the origin of the Green Man, but it is obvious
that he was some kind of wood-spirit. There are a large number
in the region around the Quantock Hills in Somerset – hills which
were thickly wooded in the past. Some of the heads have
intertwining branches growing from their mouths with birds
perching in them. At Crowcombe, a carving of about 1534 has a
head with grapes growing from its mouth and two mermen
coming from its ears. Instead of hair, the man has scales on his
head. He looks like some Roman carvings of a god called
Oceanus and so it is possible that the wood-carvers got the idea
for their work from Roman carvings they had seen.

Strange Carvings
There is one type of carving which seems to have no connection
with Christianity at all, and which is unlikely to have been used
simply for decoration. This is the naked figure of a man or
woman with a tiny body and large head. Some of them were
removed from churches about a hundred years ago because the
Victorians thought they were crude. One or two still remain, but
nobody knows why they are there. Probably the best example is

Sheelagh-na-gig, **Church of St Mary and St David, Kilpeck, Hereford and Worcester.**

the female figure on a corbel on the outside of the chancel at Kilpeck in Hereford and Worcester. Figures like this are sometimes given the name *sheelagh-na-gig*. They may have been carved by masons as a kind of joke, but this seems improbable. A more likely explanation is that they were the kind of decorations used in pagan temples. The Christian Church borrowed pagan ideas until it developed its own particular art.

Fonts and the New Birth

The New Testament tells us that people were baptised when they became Christians. This ceremony usually involved dipping the person in a river or pool. The first Christians in Britain were baptised in rivers. Later, when the church was established in the country, small chapels called baptisteries were built. Some of them were built near to pagan wells and made use of the water flowing from them. Eventually, however, churches used large stone basins called fonts. Ancient fonts are very large because people sometimes actually got into the font to be baptised. Later on, when it was the custom to baptise babies, they were dipped in the water.

Two main reasons are given for baptism. The first is that it is an action which shows that the person being baptised has been 'born again'. He or she has changed his or her way of life and become a new person, and wants to show this by being baptised.

65

After being 'washed' on the inside, in the act of baptism the person is washed on the outside.

The second point of view is that the act of baptism brings about the new birth. In other words, when a person is baptised something happens to him or her and he becomes Christian. This was the view of most people while Christianity was spreading in early Britain. They thought that in some mysterious way the person dipped in the water was given a new life. Such an idea would not be strange to pagans who worshipped river gods and had sacred springs. For them, water was a powerful substance which gave life to all things.

It is not surprising that the font was seen as a kind of womb in which the new birth took place. The priest would pray for God's blessing on the water and then breathe onto it. Once a year, at Easter, an unusual and surprising ceremony took place. A very large candle, called the Paschal candle, was brought to the font. In Salisbury Cathedral the Paschal candle was eleven metres high and weighed 740 kilograms. It was raised over the font and dipped into the water three times, plunging deeper each time. Quite often churches today have a single candle standing near to the font and it is usually explained as symbolizing the light which Christ brought into the world.

At the Reformation in the sixteenth century the idea of the new birth happening at baptism was rejected along with the idea of holy water. Orders were given to remove the locks from font lids. Before this, the lids of fonts had been padlocked to prevent people stealing the holy water which they sometimes used for witchcraft and magic. If you see a font with a damaged rim, it most probably dates from before the Reformation.

Festivals

The New Testament does not give much indication of the time of the birth of Jesus. The story involves shepherds watching their sheep in the hills, so it is unlikely that it took place in the depths of winter. The earliest reference to the keeping of the Christmas festival is as late as the fourth century. Most people assume that the midwinter solstice (shortest day), which was celebrated in pagan Rome on December 25th, was adopted as the birthday of Jesus when Christianity became the official religion of the empire.

Christmas customs also reflect the pagan past. The decoration of the home with evergreens, for instance, has more to do with Anglo-Saxon Yule celebrations than Christianity, and on occasions it has been condemned by the Church. The use of mistletoe is also interesting. The druids thought that the white berries contained the life-giving fluid of the tree, and they were used in fertility rituals. Our present practice of using a sprig of mistletoe as a licence to kiss may be a pale reflection of the earlier custom.

Easter celebrates the death and resurrection of Jesus Christ. The name 'Easter' is not a Christian word, but comes from the Anglo-Saxon *Eosturmonath*, the fourth month, named after the spring goddess *Eostre*. The custom of giving eggs at Easter comes from pre-Christian times and is part of the general celebration of the return of life in the springtime. It is interesting to note that Jews have an egg on the *seder* table at Passover, which more or less coincides with Easter.

Rogation Days in the Christian calendar replaced the pagan *Robigalia*. On April 25th, church congregations would walk in procession through the fields of the parish asking for God's blessing on the crop. Churches in some parts of Britain still take part in ceremonies connected with the blessing of springs and wells. The wells at Tissington in Derbyshire are dressed with flowers for Ascension Day; other Derbyshire wells are dressed later in the year.

The Feast of Saint John the Baptist was held on the day of the midsummer solstice. This is because John was born six months earlier than Jesus, according to the gospel story. In France, the day is called *Les Feux de la Saint Jean*, and, following a pagan Celtic tradition, fires are lit on the tops of hills and people dance around them.

Harvest was an important time in a community which depended on farming for its survival. Several earlier customs seem to have been adopted by the Church. In particular, there is the custom of bringing a sheaf of wheat, or even a corn dolly, into the church. Nowadays the act is mainly decorative, but in the past it had a deeper significance.

In ancient times it was believed that wheat grew because of the influence of a corn-goddess. Her life went into the growing stalks and made them develop and ripen. When harvest came, the stalks were cut by the reapers and the life was taken from them. Gradually as the workers moved across the field the power of the corn-goddess was concentrated into fewer and fewer stalks. When only enough for one sheaf was left, it was carefully cut and used to make a corn dolly, the image of the corn-goddess. She was

Corn dolly making.

then carefully preserved until the following spring when she was ploughed back into the earth. The idea that corn dollies bring luck reflects this earlier belief.

The Influence of the Dead

October 31st was the end of the Celtic year and the start of *Samhain*. At this time, as we saw in the last chapter, it was thought that the dead returned to make contact with the living. The Christian Church created two festivals at which the dead were to be remembered. They were All Saints Day (November 1st) and All Souls Day (November 2nd). In some places it is the custom to light candles and place them on the graves of relatives and friends at this time of the year.

The idea of praying for the dead is common in some Christian traditions, as is the idea that certain dead people are able to hear and answer the prayers of the living. At one time the churches would be crowded on All Saints Day as people queued to stand in front of the bones of dead saints asking them for favours. In Britain most of these shrines and their relics have gone, but in one or two places some have managed to survive.

68

At Whitchurch Canonicorum in Dorset there is a Medieval shrine containing the bones of an Anglo-Saxon martyr called Saint Wit. Her bones are in a stone coffin which rests on a large stone altar which has three oval holes in it. In the past, pilgrims seeking the help of Saint Wit would put injured parts of their body through the holes in the hope that the dead saint would heal them. On one occasion at a different tomb an eager pilgrim climbed through the holes and could not get out. The clergy had to dismantle the shrine!

People visiting the shrine of Saint Wit today will notice that money is thrown through the holes. Such a custom seems to reflect the belief that offerings made to the gods would benefit the living. This is what they did at Neolithic chambered tombs and at Celtic holy wells.

Reformers and Puritans

Not all Christians have been happy about the Church's contact with paganism. They think that the beliefs and practices of the Church have been too influenced by pagan beliefs. In their view, the Christian religion is something unique and very different from all other forms of religion. They have tried to avoid all forms of compromise and have used the Bible to guide them.

At the Reformation, for instance, there was an attempt to get rid of everything not taught in the Bible. Shrines and statues were broken and many festivals were removed from the Church's calendar. A hundred years later, the Puritans went even further. They stopped the celebration of Christmas and ordered that all maypoles were to be cut down (see p. 45). As far as they were concerned, religion was the response of the heart which had been renewed by the Holy Spirit. Without this spiritual rebirth, they argued, men and women were blind to the truth about God and their religious beliefs were bound to be false. Today the thunder of the Reformation is only faintly heard and the old gods are still with us.

Anyone visiting an old church or cathedral will see scars of former conflicts of this kind. There are niches where statues once stood and statues which have lost heads or noses. Stone altars are used as doorsteps and tiny pieces of shattered windows have been put together in a jumble. Often high in the chancel there are doorways which seem to lead nowhere; the screens to which they led have been taken away and burned.

Conclusion

When Christianity came to Britain, the old beliefs did not die. Ordinary people could not read or write and for them the new religion would have been little more than a variation of the old one. Many of them still worshipped in the same temples, which, with a few changes, were now called churches. They still had holidays on the same festivals, though they were given different names. Some of the old priests were now wearing different clothes and were acting as ministers of the Church.

Obviously this was not the case everywhere. For many men and women the Gospel was good news and they turned from their old beliefs which they now saw as false and accepted Jesus Christ as their Saviour. As far as they were concerned, Christianity was something totally new. This was so in the case of great leaders like Saint Patrick, and many today still look upon Christianity as unique. Others take a broader view and find glimpses of truth in all religions.

Revision Exercise

1 Name four gods after whom the days of the week are named.
2 What does the word 'rood' mean?
3 Where are Green Men most commonly found in English parish churches?
4 What happened on Rogation Days in many parishes?
5 Why did the Reformers do so much damage in churches?

Things to Do

1 Find out what you can about Christmas and Easter customs, such as Yule logs, holly and ivy, Easter eggs, Hot Cross buns, mistletoe.
2 Find out what you can about iconoclasm (image-breaking) in the sixteenth and seventeenth centuries.
3 Collect the names of pub signs and see how many of them reflect ancient beliefs.
4 Study John 3:1–10 and discuss the meaning of the 'new birth'. See also 1 Peter 1:23–25; Titus 3:3–7.

Encyclopaedia Britannica, **Articles for Further Study**

'Feasts and Festivals', Macropaedia, Vol. 7, p. 197–202.
'Western Christian Medieval Art', Macropaedia, Vol. 19, p. 345–379.

8 Saint Michael and the Dragon

Nearly all churches in Britain are dedicated to someone and quite often the dedication chosen can tell us something about the beliefs of the people who built the church. In this chapter we shall be thinking about one dedication in particular – Saint Michael – because he was often chosen when a church was built on a pagan holy place. There are in fact over seven hundred churches of Saint Michael in Britain and 611 of them were built before the Reformation. This represents about one in every twenty churches in the country.

Churches were first dedicated to saints and angels in the fourth century. It was done because people believed that the person chosen would protect the church and its congregation. The angel Michael was chosen because they thought that he was able to fight and conquer Satan. To understand what this means it is necessary to look at the last and most puzzling book of the Bible, the Book of Revelation.

The Book of Revelation

The Revelation to Saint John is a series of visions. Most of them are very strange and difficult to understand. In the twelfth chapter of the book there is a description of a war in heaven between two armies of angels: good angels under the leadership of Michael and evil angels under the leadership of the dragon.

> Now a war arose in heaven, Michael and his angels fighting against the dragon; and the dragon and his angels fought, but they were defeated and there was no longer any place for them in heaven. And the great dragon was thrown down, that ancient serpent, who is called the Devil and Satan, the deceiver of the whole world – he was thrown down to the earth, and his angels were thrown down with him.

Revelation 12:7–9

When the Book of Revelation was written, and until as recently as the early sixteenth century, people believed that the earth was the centre of the universe and that the sky was like a dome over the earth. Heaven was above the sky and the sun, moon and stars moved across the dome of the sky. Beyond heaven there was nothing. What is described in the Book of Revelation was, therefore, easy to visualize. Satan and his evil angels, with nowhere else to go, had come down into the space below the dome of heaven and in that position they had direct access to men and women.

Good and bad angels were thought to be intelligent creatures without bodies. The idea of invisible evil spirits in the sky above them was, therefore, frightening for the people of the Middle Ages. They took the power of the devil and his angels very seriously. They thought that all around them were invisible spirits waiting to deceive, waiting to entice men away from the worship of God in heaven. The apostle Paul expressed their fears in words he wrote to the people of Ephesus:

> Put on the whole armour of God, that you may be able to stand against the wiles of the devil. For we are not contending with flesh and blood, but against the principalities, against the powers, against the world rulers of this present darkness, against the spiritual hosts of wickedness in the heavenly places.

Ephesians 6:10–12

Paul is saying that Christians need not fear men on earth; their real enemies are the armies of evil angels all about them. Whenever a person began to worship sun, moon or stars, or any other god, they had been deceived by the Devil. When, therefore, Christianity converted these people and their temple to the worship of the one true God, it was necessary to call on the strong protection of good angels to defend them and their church. Whenever there is a pre-Reformation dedication to Saint Michael, we can be fairly sure that there was a pagan holy place nearby.

Conversion of Pagan Temples
We have already referred to the conversion of holy places to the new religion. One early Christian who encouraged this was Mellitus, a seventh-century Archbishop of Canterbury, who had been sent to Britain as a missionary by Pope Gregory I. Mellitus gave the following instructions:

I have, on mature deliberation on the affair of the English, determined that the temples of the idols in that nation ought not to be destroyed, but that the idols in them be destroyed.

One of the earliest pagan temples to be converted in this way was in Brittany. It was on the summit of the impressive Mont St Michel, which at that time was joined to the mainland and surrounded by dense woods. In 709 a Christian church was established on the summit. Similar hill-tops in Britain came to have chapels dedicated to Saint Michael built on them; probably the best example being Saint Michael's Mount, near Marazion in Cornwall.

Dedications to Saint Michael in Britain are associated particularly with hill-tops, headlands and springs, and they tend to be concentrated in the south-west of the country. The most westerly is Chapel Carn Brea, just above the airfield near Lands End. When looked at from below, the hill on which the chapel once stood is not impressive, but from the top the view is surprisingly good. On top of the hill there are traces of prehistoric cairns and below it, in three directions, there are standing stones. Set into one of the natural boulders on top of the hill is a metal plaque commemorating the fact that Margaret Keturah Fulleylove Thornley, 'servant of Michael', began her pilgrimage to all the Saint Michael sites in Europe from that spot. This is one of the many pieces of evidence that people today are still interested in the power of the angel Michael or of the sacred places he guards.

Between Indians Queens and Bodmin, on the edge of the moon-like landscape formed by the china clay spoil heaps of southern Cornwall, there is a precipitous crag called Roche Rock. It rises sheer from the bracken-covered field below, and perched precariously on its top is the ruined chapel of Saint Michael. To ascend the rock today there are conveniently placed iron rungs set into the rock face. There must have been a compelling reason for building the chapel there in the fourteenth century.

Out of sight of Roche Rock, on the other side of Bodmin Moor, is an even more impressive church which stands on a rocky crag almost 400 metres above sea level. Visible for miles around, the church of Saint Michael de Rupe, or 'of the rock', was built about 1130 on the site of what appears to have been a hill-fort. It seems a strange place to build a church. For centuries wedding and funeral parties have struggled up the rough track to the summit of Brent Tor, often against fierce winds. The summit is so rocky that it was often difficult to find enough depth for the coffins. Also, strange as it may seem, they often found springs when they were digging the graves – another reason why this place would have been chosen by the Celts as a sanctuary.

Further up the country, and lying almost in line with the other hill-top churches already mentioned, is Burrow Mump, a prominent hillock rising out of the Somerset plain a few miles north-east of Taunton. On top of the mound stands the ruined church of Saint Michael. This is the country of King Alfred and not far away is the site of Athelney Abbey. The Mump was used as a *motte* for a Norman keep in the twelfth century and the church was built there in the fifteenth century.

Ten miles further along the road to the north-east there is the 158 metre-high Glastonbury Tor, dominated by the solitary tower of Saint Michael. This is the area of ancient Avalon which has a history that goes back to Celtic times. Few places in Britain are surrounded by so many legends and so much romance. It was here, says one story, that Joseph of Arimathea brought the holy grail – the cup used by Jesus at the Last Supper with his disciples. Here he planted his staff and it took root. The thorn tree which flowers at Christmas is thought to have been grown from a shoot from the original tree. More firmly grounded in history are its connections with Saint Patrick and Celtic Christianity.

The great abbey of Saint Dunstan, built in the tenth century and enlarged in the twelfth and thirteenth centuries, surprises visitors by its size. It shows the importance of this small town in the past. But many who come to Glastonbury do so for the effect of the place on them, not for its ruins. There is, they claim, a magic in Glastonbury. Hundreds gather on the Tor to see the midsummer sunrise; many more visit the holy spring in Chalice Well Garden. Some who come are Christians of the Orthodox, Catholic and Protestant traditions; many more are interested in the old religion and Glastonbury is a centre for such groups as the *Lost Knowledge Organization* and the *Pagan Life Society*. It must be one of the few towns in the country with a pub sign saying 'Hippies Not Admitted'.

Within sight of Glastonbury Tor to the south-east is Saint Michael's Mount, Montacute. The story of this hill-top sanctuary dates from the time of King Cnut (*c.* 944–1035). According to legend, a local blacksmith had a dream in which Christ appeared to him and told him to dig at the top of the *mons acutus* near the village. At first he ignored the dream, but he had it again and was frightened. He met the local priest and with a group of other men they dug on the hill and found a large stone. Suddenly the stone broke in two and inside they found a crucifix of shining black flint. The chapel of Saint Michael was built on the spot. Today a tower stands where the chapel once stood.

Michael churches are also found near to springs and rivers. The church of Askerswell in Dorset, for instance, is near to the source of a stream which feeds the River Brit. It is also between two Iron Age hill-forts: Eggardon Hill and Chilcombe Hill. Further to the east, in an area rich in standing stones and burial mounds, Saint Michael's at Winterbourne Steepleton stands close to the fast-flowing Winterbourne. Higher up the valley, which is known locally as Bride Valley, there is an oval ring of stones standing close to the source of the stream. Just over the hill to the east is yet another Saint Michael dedication, also near to a fast flowing stream, and below this is situated the Romano-British temple inside the ramparts of Maiden Castle. In other parts of the country there are Saint Michael churches near to hill-forts. Perhaps the early Christians associated all hill-forts with paganism?

The Welsh word for Michael is *Mihangel*, and churches dedicated to the angel are usually called Llanfihangel. Some of the churches are now disused because of lack of interest or movement of the population. At least one of them, however, seemed to revert to the religion of the pre-Christian site. This particular church stood redundant in a remote valley with its door padlocked, unused until it was taken over by a group of hippies in 1975.

Local tradition says that the people living in this high mountain valley were descended from the fairies. This fact, coupled with the Michael dedication, may have attracted the hippies. In the east window of the church, above the altar in the place usually reserved for a cross, they placed a large slate on which was a painting of what appeared to be a male/female figure bearing a child.

Ley Lines
Much recent interest in Saint Michael churches has centred on the alleged alignment of the sites. It is claimed that pagan holy places were situated along lines of power to which the prehistoric people were sensitive. The Christian churches have helped to preserve

these lines for us. If sites like those mentioned above are marked on a large-scale map, they do appear to lie in straight lines. Around Glastonbury Tor, for instance, there are at least five Saint Michael dedications which seem to lie in a line. When one looks closely, however, the lines are not absolutely straight. In fact, the longest so-called 'ley line' which runs from Saint Michael's Mount in Cornwall to Avebury in Wiltshire misses most sites said to be on it by several miles. Also, many of the sites are on natural hills. The ley-line theory demands the belief that the geography of Britain has been affected by these lines of force.

Though accurate map-work does not support the belief in a National Grid of ley-lines criss-crossing the country, there is clear evidence for straight lines of short runs dating from the Neolithic period. Many of the standing stones in the Penwith district of Cornwall are exactly in line. On Exmoor, three circles (Withypool Hill, Porlock Common and Almsworthy Common) are exactly in line, though several miles apart. The four large henges at Priddy – each has a diameter of about 180 metres – are in a line over 1,200 metres long.

The least shown by these alignments is an interest on the part of early man in straight lines, and this interest is not confined to Britain. In recent years there has been much work done on the straight lines marked out on the ground in the Andes mountains of South America. Around Nazca and Cusco there are hundreds of lines scratched out of the rough surface of the desert soil or the mountain slope which extend for miles. They run in all directions and go over the tops of high ridges and eventually end on a hill-top. What is interesting is that several Spanish mission churches are built on these lines, presumably on the sites of Indian holy places. The lines do not seem to have astronomical significance; the natives apparently wanted to join up just hills, springs and stones thought to be homes of the gods.

The angel Michael is also important in Judaism. In the book of Daniel Michael comes to Daniel's aid (Daniel 10:10–21), and for this reason he is looked on as the guardian angel of the Jewish people. When Simon Marks chose 'Saint Michael' as the brand-name for Marks and Spencer, he had this idea in mind. Michael was also his father's name.

Dragon-killers
The church has taken a great interest in the dragon-killing ability of Saint Michael, and many churches have decorations which

Above, **tympanum showing St George and dragon, Brinsop Church, Hereford and Worcester;** *right*, **bench-end, Withersfield Church, Suffolk.**

incorporate dragons. When the carving or picture shows a dragon-killer with wings, then the subject is Michael. If it is a man in armour without wings, then it will be Saint George, the patron saint of England. If the figure is female, then it will be the third dragon-killing saint honoured by the church: Saint Margaret. She was the eleventh-century wife of King Malcolm III of Scotland.

The reputations of George and Margaret as dragon-killers seem to have arisen at about the same time in the late twelfth century, and they appear to have gained these reputations because of their bravery in the face of paganism. George, like Michael, is usually

77

shown killing the dragon with a spear or sword; Margaret kills her dragon by poking the long shaft of a cross down its throat.

The church of All Saints, Trull, which is supposed to lie on the line running from Avebury to Saint Michael's Mount in Cornwall, has a triple Medieval window showing the three dragon-killers side by side. It was made in the late fifteenth century and has one feature which is usually missed by the visitor.

Each of the windows has a border of small pieces of glass. Michael's border consists of small crowns; George's has small fleur-de-lis. The centre window, however, which shows Margaret, has twenty-four Green Men, each with foliage coming from mouth and ears. The fact that the windows have different borders suggests that the artist connected the design of the border with the figure in the window. If this is so, then why has Margaret got a border of Green Men? Do they represent the paganism which she opposed?

There is another detail which seems to be important. Margaret's dress is covered with seventeen five-point stars. In Medieval imagery, the five-point star, or pentacle, was associated with a number of things including the five Christian virtues. The pentacle was worn by Sir Gawain when he fought the Green Knight (see p. 26). The artist seems to be telling us that Saint Margaret killed the dragon, that is the false religion, through the quality of her life.

The following is taken from *Sir Gawain and the Green Knight*, but 'her' has been substituted for 'that fine man':

Liberality and Lovingkindness . . .
Continence and Courtesy which were never corrupted;
And Piety, the surpassing virtue. These pure five
Were more firmly fixed on her
Than on any other . . .

Sir Gawain and the Green Knight, translated by B. Stone

Conclusion
Church dedications often tell us something about the history of the building. The saint chosen, for instance, might be the one who founded the church. Saint Michael dedications are particularly interesting because most of them are very old and were given to churches which were built on the sites of pagan temples.

Legends about dragons are also common and they too tell us about early beliefs. Saint Margaret, wife of King Malcolm III of Scotland, is remembered as a dragon-killer, probably because of her opposition to paganism. The purity of her life was in contrast with the lax morals of her pagan contemporaries.

Revision Exercise
1 What kinds of churches were chosen for dedication to Saint Michael?
2 Name three famous churches dedicated to Saint Michael in Britain.
3 What does the word Llanfihangel mean?
4 What can you say about the 'lines' of Nazca and Cusco?
5 What are the five Christian virtues? Explain them in your own words.

Things to Do
1 Discuss whether religion should make people good.
2 Find out whether there are any churches dedicated to Saint Michael near to you. Were they built on or near a pagan holy place? Try to arrange a visit.
3 Mark ancient churches, burial mounds, holy wells, standing stones, etc. on an Ordnance Survey map and see whether any of them lie in a straight line. A good way to mark the map neatly is with a red ball pen and a radius aid.
4 Borrow a copy of *Sir Gawain and the Green Knight*. What do lines 623–665 and 2160–2211 tell us about Medieval belief?
5 Study the New Testament teaching about angels: Matthew 1:20, 24; 2:13, 19; Luke 1:26–38; Acts 5:19; 2 Peter 2:4, 11; Jude 6; 1 Corinthians 6:3; Revelation 12:1–9.

9 Field Study at Ancient Religious Sites

The closest we can get to the early religions of Britain is to visit sacred sites. Reading about them and looking at photographs obviously helps, but there is no substitute for actually visiting the places. Pictures cannot convey much of the atmosphere of a place, and the atmosphere is important. Even a single standing stone in its authentic setting can create an awareness in us. It may not be an awareness of the gods of the past, but it is a step in that direction. That particular stone was chosen to stand in that particular place. It expresses the beliefs of people who died long ago and it can help us to understand their beliefs.

We know from our own experience that we do things best when we are interested in what we are doing. There must be an emotional involvement. If we are doing some homework, for instance, little effort is needed if we are interested in what we are doing. When there is no interest, then we sometimes have to force ourselves to do it. Any emotion, whether it is love, joy, curiosity, fear, anxiety, or any other, will put us in the right frame of mind to do what we have to do. When we stand next to a standing stone, therefore, or in a cathedral, then we might be able to imagine the kind of emotional involvement the builders had. This is a necessary step towards the understanding of the religion of these early people.

Visits to places of religious interest can be rewarding from purely the point of view of the scenery. Stone Age monuments are often situated in impressive places. Whether it is Carn Gloose Burial Chamber on the cliffs above Cape Cornwall, or Castle Rigg Stone Circle in the mountains of Cumbria, the scenery is breath-taking.

Some of the monuments may be off the beaten track, but the walk is nearly always worthwhile. Even if the prospect from below seems unpromising when visiting a hill-fort, for instance, it is best to persevere because the ascent of a few metres can improve the view considerably. A visit to Capel Garmon Burial Chamber, near Betws-y-Coed, for instance, gives a panoramic view of the Snowdon range of mountains which is as good as any, yet from the map the site appears to have little to offer.

The most interesting sites are unfortunately distributed unevenly over the country. Some areas have a high concentration of monuments, such as Salisbury Plain, whereas others apparently have few. In this chapter, guidance is given concerning the location of interesting places in any part of the country so that visits can be arranged. Even if you live in large towns and cities you will have parish churches on your doorstep and most schools now have a minibus so that trips can be taken further afield. Stonehenge, for instance, is only two hours' drive away from inner London on the M3 and A303.

Enthusiasts will want to organize field trips to areas rich in religious sites. Alternatively, individuals may like to plan holiday routes with their parents via some of the monuments. Long journeys can be made easier if there are occasional breaks to visit a cool ancient church or to stroll across a few fields to a burial chamber. The following remarks may seem obvious but they should be made.

1 If the monument is not on a public right of way, then it is important to ask permission to cross it from the owner of the land. Public rights of way are usually clearly marked on Ordnance Survey maps.

2 Because of the increasing number of thefts from churches, it may be necessary to borrow a key to unlock a church door. There should be a notice telling you where the key can be obtained. If there is not a notice, then it is best to contact the local vicar, who should live fairly near to the church. Do not go to the nearest house unless it is clearly marked 'Vicarage' or 'Rectory'. If you know in advance that you want to visit a particular church, then the name and address of the vicar of that parish can be found in a copy of Crockford's Clerical Directory, which should be available in the public library.

3 Be prepared for mud even if the weather is dry. It can be frustrating getting within sight of a monument only to be stopped by a large puddle or stretch of mud.

4 Two useful items for visits to old churches are a pair of binoculars and a torch. Some of the interesting features, such as roof-bosses, may be high in the roof. A torch may be useful to see a carving in a dark place, for example on a bench-end.

Finding Sites on Ordnance Survey Maps

Most ancient sites are marked on maps in old-fashioned Gothic type. There are, however, some inconsistencies and sometimes they are marked in plain type. It may also be helpful to study different editions of the same map because changes are sometimes made and an ancient site marked on one edition may be dropped from another. It is also necessary to check precisely the location of a site. The word 'Long Barrow', for instance, may cover about half a mile of fields, and so it is important to find the right dot or mark representing the long barrow. Sometimes antiquities are marked with a cross and the position is clear. If there is no cross, then a magnifying glass helps to distinguish the various dots which may be near to the relevant word.

The most popular Ordnance Survey maps are the 1:50,000 series, which has a scale of about 1¼ inches to the mile. For finding remote standing stones or crosses, however, the 1:25,000 series is much better. This larger-scale map shows hedges and field boundaries. It is much easier to find a monument if you know which side of a hedge it stands.

The Ordnance Survey also publish several maps of archaeological interest which concentrate on specific periods of history. They include:

Ancient Britain: there are two sheets (north and south) which show over a thousand of the visible ancient sites in Britain which were built before 1066. Most of them are of religious interest.

Southern Britain in the Iron Age: this map covers the period from about 700 BC to AD 100.

Roman Britain: covers from AD 43 to AD 410. Amongst other things it shows the location of Roman temples throughout Britain.

Britain in the Dark Ages: covers the period from AD 410 to 871 and marks pagan and Christian places of interest.

Britain before the Norman Conquest: shows the locations of monasteries, churches and chapels.

What to Look For on Maps

The great variety of religious sites which can be seen in Britain

82

has been made clear. Those which can be found on maps are:

Churches: these are marked with a cross. Churches with towers or spires have an additional black square or circle under the cross. It is easy to miss the small cross of a church without tower or spire, yet some of these buildings are very interesting. Kilpeck, for instance, has neither tower nor spire, but it is among the most fascinating buildings in Britain.

Tumuli: this term includes all types of round barrows. It will be necessary to refer to specialist books if specific types of round barrows are to be visited. Look out for groups of barrows and see whether they follow the lines of a ridge. Barrows with names are usually more prominent than others.

Long barrows: no distinction is made between earthen long barrows and those with chambered tombs inside.

Standing stones: those with names are usually impressive. It is important to note that not all stones are marked on the 1:50,000 series of maps.

Forts: usually Iron Age hill-forts. Some of them were not occupied and may have been storage areas. Others were hill-top temples. Forts of all kinds are usually worth a visit because of the view.

Wells: either named or in Gothic type. Often there is much more than just a hole in the ground.

Trees: Gospel Oaks and other named trees may be significant, even though they may not be very old. They probably stand on the spot where an ancient holy tree stood.

Crosses: usually marked in Gothic type and often no more than a stump. In Celtic areas (Cornwall, Wales, Scotland) the crosses are usually impressive because they were made of stone too hard for the image-breakers to smash.

Useful Reference Books
The availability of books obviously varies from library to library. In most public libraries there will be a section of books of local

interest. It is always a good idea to ask at the counter in case local history books are kept in a separate section or store. Also, always remember to look in the 'Oversize' section of books. Some of the best books are in this section.

The following titles are recommended for those who want to plan ahead. When you decide on a particular area of interest you can start to list the things you want to see.

An Inventory of Ancient Monuments (London, 1911 onwards). Unfortunately these superb books cover only a few areas in Britain. They are published by HMSO and describe everything from ancient boundary stones to the carvings in churches. Seven large volumes cover the county of Dorset alone.

The Buildings of England by Nikolaus Pevsner (Harmondsworth: Penguin, 1951). Volumes cover the counties of England and list every important building, including megalithic monuments.

The King's England by Arthur Mee (London: Hodder and Stoughton, 1937 onwards). This book gives an account of the things worth seeing in every town and village. There is much useful information on what to see in churches.

Penguin Guide to Prehistoric England and Wales by James Dyer (Harmondsworth: Penguin, 1981).

Shell County Guides, edited by John Betjeman and John Piper (London: Faber and Faber, 1971 onwards).

Place-names
Just as the days of the week are named after gods, so many places in Britain are named after the gods with which they are associated. It is a useful exercise to look up local place-names in a dictionary of place-names to find clues to the pre-Christian past. Bilston, for example, on the edge of the Black Country may seem an unlikely place for a Celtic sanctuary. Its name, however, may be derived from *Beal-tuinn* or *Bil-tuinn*, meaning 'the fire of Beal', the sun-god. Beacon Hill, therefore, one of those unpromising hills from below, may be the site of a Celtic sanctuary dedicated to the sun. A few miles to the east, over as industrial a scene as it is possible to get, stands Wednesbury church on a high hill: it may be connected with Woden.

Below are listed a few names which are important clues in the search for ancient religious sites:

Woden: (Wednesbury, Wednesfield, Woodnesborough) places where Woden or Odin may have been worshipped
Thor: (Thunderfield) sanctuary of Thor or Thunor
Tiw: (Tysoe, Tuesley) sanctuaries of Tiw or Tyw
Frig: (Fridaythorpe) possibly a sanctuary of the fertility goddess
beorg: means 'mound' or 'barrow'. In some cases it may refer to a sacred mound, as in Woodnesborough above.
hearg: pagan shrine, from which we get Harrow-on-the-Hill, the place where cattle were killed in November and offered to the gods.
weoh: also refers to a pagan temple, as in Weedon – hill with a temple on it.

Other names which are worth following up are those which include:

Devil: as in Devil's Bed and Bolster, a megalithic tomb.
Arthur: as in Arthur's Stone, a chambered tomb.
Robin Hood: as in Robin Hood's Butts, a group of round barrows.

So too, names which include 'holy', 'giant', 'fairy', 'grove'.

What to Look For at a Megalithic Site
It is very easy to visit a megalithic site, take a quick look and feel disappointed. Many people visit Avebury, for instance, and do not take the trouble to walk around the perimeter of the main circle. They spend hours travelling to and from the place, but only a few minutes actually looking at it.

In the case of a ring of stones, there is something to be gained by walking around it and looking at each stone individually, noting the shape and texture. Are the stones made of the same kind of rock? Some circles have one stone made of a different material from all the rest. Boscawen-noon circle in Cornwall, for example, has one stone made of quartz. The circles at Stanton Drew are made of three different types of rock which was quarried in different places in the area. What reasons might they have had for using stone from different sources?

It is also worthwhile to walk around the stones at a distance from them, looking at the monument as a whole, and also looking beyond it at the neighbouring fields and horizon. There may be an unmarked stone in a field or bump on the horizon which is related to the monument.

Finally, it is always a good idea to look on the ground in any place where the soil may be eroded or where rabbits or moles have been at work. It may be possible to find a worked flint or a piece of broken pottery. On no account must the search for such objects be anything other than a surface search, nor must it be on private land without permission.

If anything is found which looks unusual or interesting, then the exact location must be remembered and it should be shown to someone at a museum. The best thing to do is to take home anything which could be man-made and then wash it and clean it with an old toothbrush. When it is dry, the grid reference to the spot where it was picked up can be written on it with a mapping pen and white indian ink. It is a mistake not to mark finds of this kind straightaway, because it is easy to forget exactly where a piece of flint or pottery was found.

What to Look For in Old Churches
Only pre-Reformation churches are of interest to those looking for traces of the old religion. It should be noted, however, that many new churches have been rebuilt on the foundations of older ones and much of the old building material may have been used in the fabric of the new one. It is always best to go in and have a look, even if the exterior looks fairly recent.

The first thing to note is the setting. Is it near to a stream or spring? Is it on a mound or near to an earthwork? Are there any natural boulders which have been left in the churchyard? If there are, see if you can find out why they have been left there. Then look at the shape of the windows and doors. This should give an indication of the age of the building, unless it is a modern copy of an earlier style of architecture. The building will probably fall into one of the following categories:

Anglo-Saxon: these churches are rare because most churches built before the Norman conquest were made of wood. Some churches do still have Saxon fonts and pieces of Saxon carved masonry.

Romanesque: this was the style of architecture of the eleventh and twelfth centuries. It is heavy and solid and copied from the Roman buildings which were still standing. Doors and windows

86

Left, Saxon tower, Earls Barton, Northamptonshire; *right*, Romanesque doorway, Church of St Mary and St David, Kilpeck, Hereford and Worcester. There is a Green Man on the right-hand pillar capital.

are rounded and often decorated with chevrons, zig-zags and cable-moulding. Carvings are often grotesque and incorporate features which seem more pagan than Christian. One reason for this may be that the masons had not yet had time to develop art-forms which were thoroughly Christian. On the other hand, some imagery may have been used deliberately to bridge the gap between the old religion and the new.

Gothic: many consider this to be the finest style of Christian architecture ever produced, although the name was originally given by those who thought it was the work of Goths, that is, barbarians. It was used from the thirteenth to the sixteenth centuries, and then revived in the nineteenth. It made use of pointed arches for windows and doors. Compared with the Romanesque style it is spacious and light. This is mainly due to the fact that pointed arches can safely span wider gaps than round arches. Carvings are fine and lifelike. The cruder pagan elements are rarely used and, when they are, it is usually in high places such as on roof-bosses. In some areas the ends of benches (pews)

87

are decorated with carvings which seem to have little to do with Christianity.

The Gothic style is usually divided into three periods: Early English, Decorated and Perpendicular. The last style is found only in Britain and is often extremely beautiful.

On entering a church, pause to examine the door. Often an old door is concealed in a more recent porch. Some Romanesque doors have a semicircular block of stone filling in the round bit of the arch. It is called a tympanum, and often has a rich carving on it. Notice also the columns on either side of the door. Early Norman doors sometimes have snakes on the top of the left-hand pillar.

Inside the door you will probably find the font. If it is decorated at all, then examine the whole of the decoration. Sometimes what appears to be a uniform geometrical design may have an unusual feature almost hidden in it. Some early Norman fonts have details which cannot be Christian.

If the pews are old, then look at their ends for carvings. Once again, it is best to examine them all, because there may be an old carving in a side aisle in the middle of a section of new ones. Sitting on the floor often gives the best view.

Many of the best bench-ends were carved between about 1500 and 1540 and occasionally you will find one that is dated. Most of the designs are Christian and were put there partly for the benefit of the majority in the congregation who could not read. A common design shows the Lamb of God – the figure of a lamb with a bent leg holding a cross. Another shows a pelican feeding its young from its own flesh; this represents the Christian benefiting from the death of Jesus. Some benches show scenes from Medieval Mystery plays and many others show scenes from everyday life. For the history student they are a good source of information on Medieval fashion and industry.

Some churches have fascinating pieces of wood-carving on misericords, which are the wooden projections underneath the tip-up seats used by the choir. They were put there so that the choirmen could take the weight off their legs during long services. (The word means 'compassionate'.) As they were out of sight most of the time, the wood-carver was able to exercise his imagination in some of the designs.

Old glass may be a source of information about past beliefs. Unfortunately Medieval stained glass is rare because so much of

Bench-end carved in 1534 showing men killing a two-headed dragon, Crowcombe Church, Somerset.

it was broken at the time of the Reformation. Quite often a small section of an old window is preserved in a modern window. It is best to look at the church guide to find out what glass there is. When you find the window, then look at the background detail for any interesting features.

The altar of the church is probably made of wood, because most stone altars were removed at the time of the Reformation. This was done because the Protestant emphasis was on eating bread and drinking wine at a table, rather than offering a sacrifice at an altar. Some churches do, however, retain their stone altars in the form of doorsteps or plinths. Some stone altars still have the holes which were put there so that the relics of saints which were kept in the altar stone could be seen.

89

Finally, look at the pillar capitals and the roof bosses, if there are any. Here again, it is important to look at every single pillar and section of roof. Green Men and other carvings were sometimes almost hidden from view, and they have to be searched out.

Buildings and Feelings

As has been said earlier, a building or a ring of stones is an expression of the feelings men and women have had in the past about themselves, their place in the world, and the gods or powers upon which they felt themselves to be dependent. Because they are expressions of feelings, they can also evoke feelings in us. This is why it is so important not to rush a visit. We need to take time to get to know the 'feel' of the place. It might help some to start by trying to imagine the effort involved in building the place at all. Why did they take the trouble to haul that slab of stone or those blocks of masonry all that way in the first place? Why so big? Why so high?

We cannot know what made early communities feel religious. It might help, however, to think of some of the reasons given by others for becoming religious. One writer, for instance, has spoken of a sense of longing which kept coming to him. When it came, it was as if he was reaching out for something he could not see. Is this what standing stones and church spires are doing? Are they expressions of man's attempt to reach beyond himself and his world for purpose and meaning?

Alternatively, some men and women have been led to think of God when they have become aware of their own insignificance in the vastness of the universe. Is this what the buildings are telling us? Is this why hill-tops were often chosen for sanctuaries?

It is not always easy to catch the atmosphere of a place, especially if you are with a crowd of others. It often helps if you try to concentrate on just one aspect of it. You could perhaps make a sketch of some detail that interests you. Or you might take a brass-rubbing, or a photograph of a window or bench-end. These kinds of things will remind you of the place and help you to recollect your feelings when you get home.

Glossary

Aborigine native Australian hunter and gatherer who was already settled there when Europeans first arrived

Anthropology the study of man's physical characteristics, his way of life and his beliefs

Barrow a round or long mound which covers one or more burials. Most were built in the Bronze Age, although they were used right up to the Saxon period

Boss a rounded projection covering the joints in the main supports of a vault or ceiling, usually decorated

Capital the upper part of a pillar or column

Capstone large slab of stone lying across the top of upright stones in a megalithic tomb

Constellation group of stars which may have a name

Corbel projecting block of stone which supports structure above, often decorated

Dedication the name of a saint or angel or deity associated with a church

Equinox one of the two days in the year when the sun is above the horizon for as long as it is below the horizon. Day = night

Erosion wearing away by the action of water

Extinct no longer alive anywhere

Fertility the ability to reproduce

Font bowl for holding water used in baptism, usually made of stone. Ancient fonts were large enough for a baby to be dipped in

Homo Sapiens wise man, modern man, the species to which we belong

Henge circular bank of earth with inner ditch used for religious rituals during the New Stone Age. Some henges have settings of stones, for example Stonehenge, Avebury

Metonic Cycle a nineteen year cycle of the phases of the moon, discovered by Greek astronomer Meton who lived in the 5th century BC

Misericord a small projecting ledge on the underside of a tip-up seat in the choir of a church. It provided support for tired members of a choir who had to stand for a long time

Motte a mound on which the main structure of a castle was built

Neanderthal Man extinct form of man first discovered in Neandertal Valley, near Düsseldorf in Germany. Experts do not agree on the relationship between Neanderthal Man and *Homo Sapiens*

Neopagan person who practises pagan religion today

Orientation position in relation to points of the compass. Many religious structures are oriented east/west, for example: Neolithic tombs, Jewish temples, Christian churches

Paganism religion which worships many gods. *Pagus* means 'village', hence paganism sometimes refers to the traditional religion of countrymen, not Christianity or Judaism

Phallic relating to the male sex organ. Phallic images were sometimes used in religious ceremonies which aimed at increasing fertility

Psychedelic relating to increased awareness, consciousness and sensitivity, usually as a result of taking natural or synthetic drugs

Solstice either the longest day (Midsummer) or the shortest day (Midwinter)

Index